J. E. Usher

Alcoholism and its Treatment

J. E. Usher

Alcoholism and its Treatment

ISBN/EAN: 9783337331146

Printed in Europe, USA, Canada, Australia, Japan

Cover: Foto ©Lupo / pixelio.de

More available books at **www.hansebooks.com**

BY
J. E. USHER, M.D.,
FELLOW OF THE ROYAL GEOGRAPHICAL SOCIETY OF LONDON,
FORMERLY SURGEON SUPERINTENDENT AND MEDICAL OFFICER OF HEALTH TO THE
QUEENSLAND GOVERNMENT.

NEW YORK: G. P. PUTNAM'S SONS.
LONDON: BAILLIÈRE, TINDALL & COX.
1892.

PREFACE.

ALCOHOLISM has at last attained the dignity of being styled a disease; in fact, the world of medicine has barely consented to its inclusion in the nomenclature of diseases. Not that inebriety as a form of mental disease failed to evoke the attention of the ancients, for as early as 400 years B.C. Herodotus wrote 'that both mind and body were temporarily, if not permanently, diseased following the use of alcohol.' Aristotle also laid stress upon the fact 'that drinking meant madness.' Not for one moment would I contend, however, that every man or woman who drinks is to be considered an alcoholist.

'If alcoholism is admitted to be a disease legally, what protection shall we have against the actions of persons apparently intoxicated who wish to wreak a revenge upon those they are inimical to?' This question was put to me by a gentleman well known in the literary world. I replied: 'In establishing alcoholism as a disease, it is not intended that any forms other than those of a chronic nature, or where a known heredity exists, or in which fixed mental change (insanity) is present (as shown by positive evidence in the changed conduct of an alcoholist), can be allowed in palliation of any offence; and then only where the circumstances have been fully investigated and understood. At times it would be necessary to have the opinions of experts to dispel any uncertainty that might be supposed to exist.'

There are tens of thousands who take alcohol in some shape or other daily, without apparently any great injury to their nervous or other systems. Happily these people are fortunate in possessing sufficient self-control to know when 'to put on the break' if appetite tempts them to exceed the usual allowance. Another thing not to be lost sight of is the probability that the great majority of these (as they may be called) temperate drinkers were not handicapped in any way by a degenerate constitution through transmission. Total abstinence is the ideal to be aimed at; and well may those who have attained to it cry 'Eureka.' The great work done by the magnificent organizations under the direction of the Temperance Party, although resembling somewhat the task of Sisyphus in the results obtained, is explained by the vast amount of alcoholic disease that is transmitted by heredity. If the hereditary form could be extinguished, there can hardly be a doubt about the result for the future; and the crusade against intemperance would prove easily victorious. As it is, an alcoholist may hand the disease down to even the fourth generation.

Dr. Edson, of New York, mentions a case in which a family, sprung from an intemperate mother, consisted in three generations of some twenty-seven persons, twelve of whom were addicted to the excessive use of alcoholic liquors, and three of whom used opium habitually.

What we aim at dealing with are those forms which indicate disease. A glance at the history of scientific progress reveals how much prejudice and opposition had to be contended with on the introduction of any new theory or invention. Pinel, with his suggestions as to the proper treatment of the insane, found the age very slow to accept his views. The theories of Copernicus, in relation to the position of the heavenly bodies; the laws of Kepler, as enunciated by him; the discovery of the fact that blood, and not air, circulated in the arteries, made by Harvey; and the wonderful results obtained by Jenner in his experiments to combat small-pox, all encountered opposition.

And so it has been with alcoholism, the acceptance of which as a pathological condition, is only of very recent date; and when we come to look into the matter, and realize how little it has been understood, it is not a difficult thing to comprehend why victims to the ravages of alcohol should have suffered serious neglect. Indeed, if it were not for the well-ascertained data, pointing to the vast amount of insanity that is being engendered by the use of alcohol, apart from the serious element of neurotic disease that is being transmitted to the offspring of alcoholists—and this, too, without taking into account the lessened force, both physical and mental, which is handed down to the unfortunate children—there is not the slightest shadow of a doubt but that this newly-accepted disease might continue to flourish as heretofore.

The cases of chronic alcoholism and delirium tremens treated in German hospitals during the year 1885 numbered 10,360. In Russia, as I am informed, the percentage of lunacy cases from this cause varies between 50 and 70 per cent. Here in England we find from the Reports of a Parliamentary Committee on Lunacy, issued many years ago, that the percentage of alcoholic lunatics in English asylums reached the enormous number of nearly 40 per cent. That the large number of cases of idiocy and imbecility existing is due to heredity from alcoholists is fully proven, the statistics giving from 45 to 60 per cent. It is a striking fact that a recognition of the dangers arising from the use of alcoholic liquors is the subject of special mention in the Talmud and Koran. Buddha is also very exacting, and laid down a special law interdicting the use of such beverages. In England as early as 958, in the reign of Edgar, a proclamation was issued, restricting the amount of liquor to be drunk.

A new form of inebriety has arisen in these islands, which is productive of a vast amount of insanity. I allude to the ether habit, in the North of Ireland chiefly. The Norwegians also indulge in this stimulant extensively. It is estimated that over 20,000 gallons of the liquid are consumed yearly. Recent legislation has, however, almost completely abolished this grave evil. An idea of the amount of alcohol consumed in Russia may be gained from the knowledge that the State realizes an income of 250,000,000 roubles annually from its sale.

In this work the phases of disease seen in alcoholistic conditions are illustrated by cases from the practice of many of the leading specialists in America, Great Britain, and on the Continent. A phase of the disease—and one that must be looked upon as very startling in the phenomena exhibited — is that of Alcoholic Trance. The pathological conditions surrounding, and present in, extreme forms of alcoholism have received special attention, particularly in the altered blood conditions. As the section on Treatment includes the remedies employed by some of the best-known Psychological specialists, together with those used by the author, and with very good results, some interest may attach to the knowledge that the different treatments have been compiled to date.

The analyses given at page 147 of one of the many so-called ' Bi-chloride of Gold ' remedies is taken from an address read on November 2, 1891, before the Medical Society of Chicago.

As the laws of England and America differ very much in their construction as to the mode in which alcoholists should be dealt with, a review of the same has been made. For the digests I am indebted to J. R. McIlraith, Esq., M.A., LL. B., Barrister-at-Law of the Middle Temple. I must also thank Prof. Portougaloff, Russia; Dr. Crothers, Hartford; Dr. Andrews, Chicago; Dr. Jewell, San Francisco; Drs. Weir-Mitchell and J. C. Da Costa, Philadelphia; Dr. Hammond, Washington; Drs. Cyrus Edson and Blanchard, New York; Dr. Albert Day, Boston; Dr. J. L. Gray, Indiana; Dr. Denison, Colorado; Dr. Shields, Melbourne; and Dr. Norman Kerr, of London, for much valuable assistance and information.

J. E. U.

68, WIMPOLE STREET, CAVENDISH SQUARE,
July, 1892.

CONTENTS.

	PAGE
CHAPTER I.	
PATHOLOGICAL CHANGES IN ALCOHOLISM	1
CHAPTER II.	
PATHOLOGICAL CHANGES—*continued*	5
CHAPTER III.	
ALCOHOLISM:	8
INHERITED FORM	10
ACQUIRED FORM	17
INFANTILE FORM	32
CHAPTER IV.	
INSANITY AND ALCOHOLISM	38
CHAPTER V.	
ALCOHOLIC TRANCE AND CRIME	42
CHAPTER VI.	
CEREBRAL AUTOMATISM OR TRANCE	58
CHAPTER VII.	
ALCOHOLISM AND ITS LEGAL RELATIONS	77

CHAPTER VIII.

TREATMENT OF ALCOHOLISM   PAGE 114

CHAPTER IX.

TREATMENT—*continued*   120

CHAPTER X.

TREATMENT—*continued*   126

CHAPTER XI.

ADVERTISED NOSTRUMS -   147

ALCOHOLISM AND ITS TREATMENT.

CHAPTER I.

PATHOLOGICAL CHANGES IN ALCOHOLISM.

No disease offers a better field for pathologists than the one we now have under review. Generalizing has been indulged in by a host of observers, but in very few instances can we find evidence in detail of the manifold changes existing in chronically-diseased conditions. Virchow studied the state of the blood drawn from a subject who was an alcoholist, and discovered amongst other things that 'a decrease of water and an increase of fibrin and of coloured clots' was present. Under almost precisely similar conditions other experimentalists have observed that the blood coagulates more slowly, and the fibrin found was much less than that usually present in normal blood. Coagulation may be set up by certain agents; others, again, retard or hasten it. Anything circulating in the blood, of a similar character to some of the agents just mentioned, may act in such a manner on the blood-cells and fibrin as speedily to effect coagulation. A deficiency of heart power has been known to favour this condition. Excrescences or growths in the walls of the bloodvessels may produce the same effect. Alcohol in an overwhelming quantity has been known to accomplish like changes and alterations. The affinity which this liquid has for water may in some ways explain its action, and by taking up the water in excess it is easily conceivable how much richer in fibrinous matter the blood becomes, rendering it difficult to be carried through the minute bloodvessels, and leading to the formation of clots dangerous to the circulation of the whole body.

Dr. Richardson, F.R.S., in the 'Cantor Lectures,' touching upon allied states, says: 'These facts bear on a new and refined subject of research, with which I must not trouble you further, except to add that the inquiry explains why in acute cases of poisoning by alcohol the blood is found sometimes quite fluid, at other times firmly coagulated in the vessels.' Dr. Harley, F.R.S., while working at the direct action of several toxic agents of a powerful nature many years ago, particularly with strychnine and its action on the spinal cord, found much to his surprise that even such a violent poison as strychnine, when in a state of aqueous solution, failed to produce the usual physiological effects upon the nervous organization when brought into direct contact with the nerve-cells and fibres of the exposed living spinal cord. Its toxic effects become at once evident, however, if the drug be allowed to enter the capillaries, thence into the living circulating blood. It might be imagined that the poison was brought into more immediate contact with the nervous tissue in one case than the other. This is not so, as every care was taken to inject the watery solution of strychnine into the actual substance of the spinal cord. The fact that strychnine causes convulsions when a little of it reaches the nervous system after mingling with the blood, and produces no disturbance when introduced into the nervous substance direct, led Dr. Harley to conclude that the tetanizing influence of strychnine is solely exercised through changes of a chemical nature induced in the materials of which the blood is composed. That such alteration affects the nutrition of the nerve-cells and fibres and their functions is very evident; and no doubt the tetanic spasms called into existence are mainly owing to the food material being rendered very abnormal in its properties. Dr. Harley is inclined to believe that alcohol acts in a very similar manner on the nerves through the intermediary of the blood. It has been demonstrated in some cases that a large quantity of the alcohol absorbed from the stomach is retained within the tissues of the body themselves. The late Dr. Percy found free alcohol in the brains of drinkers. In several cases, after death, I have been present when pure alcohol was obtained by simple distillation. At times the odour of alcohol on post-mortem examination is so apparent that the sense of smell need not be very acute to detect its presence. Professor Binz, of Bonn, has estimated that not more than 2·915 per cent. of the total amount of alcohol imbibed is eliminated by the skin, kidneys, and lungs. The blood of alcoholists has at times been found loaded with fatty globules. Magnus Huss was the first, I believe, to point this out.

Anæmia is not an uncommon concomitant of

alcoholism, the blood becoming very poor and watery. As may be imagined, a state of leucocythemia prevails—the white corpuscles being much in excess of their normal quantity. The liquor sanguinis is poor in albuminoids, and the salts are usually in excess. So poor in hæmoglobin may the blood become, that it is not a singular thing to find the red corpuscles reduced to 60 per 1,000 parts of blood, in contrast to 130 to 140 in the healthy state.

CHAPTER II.

PATHOLOGICAL CHANGES IN ALCOHOLISM—*continued*.

HAVING the idea that more information could be obtained from a closer investigation of the blood and of the nerve tissue (post mortem), for over two years I have, when opportunity offered, prosecuted a course of experiments having for their object the elucidation of certain points that have been and still are somewhat obscure. Repeatedly the red corpuscles were found to be irregular in outline, presenting a contracted or shrunken surface. Apparently a partial coagulation had taken place, with a decided diminution in size. It would appear that in these cases (I am speaking of advanced alcoholic disease) the alcohol has a tendency to destroy the structure of both white and red corpuscles. The chief pathological changes noted are to be found in a contraction of the red cells, with some evident exudation of the colouring matter, and an entire loss of their normal outline. The leucocytes offer a striking contrast, being more numerous; but, remarkable to say, the same utter disorganization does not appear to exist. These cells indicate that a coagulation of the nuclei has taken place, and they seem to be enlarged or swollen in a surprising degree. In healthy men such a state of things was not found to be exhibited. In anæmia we may find the corpuscles paler in colour, smaller in size, regular in outline; but I should be inclined to say that such alterations as those found in the blood of alcoholists are never met with in conditions of pure anæmia. If characteristics such as have been described are general in extreme cases of alcoholism, we can well understand how simple it is for serious morbid changes to evince their presence in the nervous matter, which, *per se*, is considered to have such an affinity for alcohol. Accepting the amount of blood in the body to equal from $\frac{1}{8}$th to $\frac{1}{10}$th of its entire weight, some significance must be attached to a partially disorganized state of so important a fluid. I have omitted to mention that the blood was less alkaline than normal in the cases tested, and the crystals were invariably augmented in quantity.

As the outcome of a number of post-mortem examinations made upon subjects addicted to alcoholism, some rather remarkable discoveries were made. Illustratively, peculiar changes were seen on some of the nerves, which in themselves appeared to have been entirely altered in structure, partaking more of the character of fibrous cords than representing bundles of nerve fibres. This state of things has, I am given to understand, been hinted at by a Continental pathologist, but so far I have not read of it. Destructive changes were observable in the cell structure of many of the terminal nerves, obviously a degeneration of protoplasm, which in turn had been replaced by a fatty material of a granular nature, and of a pronouncedly low order of vitality. At other times the nerves were found to be callous and contracted, owing to an abnormal proliferation of cell elements. Finlay speaks of the leucocytes being in excess in alcoholic paralysis, accompanied by an increase of the nuclei in the nerve sheaths. It is not uncommon after death to find the ventricles bursting with serum, this more particularly in apoplexy from intoxication.

It is hardly necessary to do more than refer to the well-known changes that occur in the bloodvessels, the liver, kidneys, and heart. Many years ago Lancereaux and Trousseau remarked 'that the appearance of the heart in alcoholism is quite special; the fat does not merely line the heart, it likewise penetrates between the muscular fibres, and induces atrophy by the compression it exerts upon them; at a later date the muscular fibres become fatty.' That the hepatic changes so commonly found, together with alterations in the structure of the spleen, may have to answer for some of the blood changes already noted is extremely likely. The origin of the blood corpuscles being still a debatable physiological point, however, some difficulty arises in fixing upon the causes of certain important phenomena. It is believed and accepted that the phagocytes, or scavengers of the blood, are almost annihilated in the systems of alcoholized persons, which means a matter of great moment should serious disease of an acute form supervene. These tiny sentinels are too weakened in numbers and strength to advance the assistance to be expected from them under healthier surroundings.

CHAPTER III.

ALCOHOLISM.

How much is conveyed by the one word heading this chapter! What a vast field of misery, poverty, and suffering is viewed by the mind, and yet how little is done to stem the tide of disease that is ever at the flood, and which, for want of proper sympathy or scientific recognition, is allowed to devastate generation after generation! A fit way of maintaining victims to perpetuate the dictum of Charles Darwin, that by a natural process the survival of the fittest is a sequence of such conditions. A spirit of false delicacy has prevailed against proper attention being given to men or women suffering from diseased conditions, the result of alcoholism, leading to the ruin and annihilation of a vaster number of persons, both physically and morally, than it would please or gratify many to understand. That we are dealing with a disease with which medicine in its broadest acceptation can cope will be clearly illustrated by giving the results of a statistical inquiry made of the patients treated at Binghampton Asylum (N.Y.), and at other places. Of 1,100 patients who had been treated at the asylum, it was found that 61 per cent. were still temperate after a period of five years. It is not too much to infer that if a large number, as is shown in the percentage given, were temperate after an interval of so lengthy a duration, they would continue temperate for the balance of their lives. Of 2,000 cases that had been treated at Fort Hamilton (N.Y.), it was ascertained that, after intervals ranging from seven to ten years, 38 per cent. were still temperate and sober.

The returns of over 3,000 cases, carefully compiled and looked into at the Washingtonian Home, Boston, revealed the fact that over 35 per cent. of *all* the cases that had been treated there were healthy and temperate after intervals ranging from eight to twelve years. In England and on the Continent the percentage of cured people varies between 32 and 41. Chronic alcoholists, as a rule, do not attain to old age. Hardly more than 1 in 400 arrives at seventy years. Some interesting data are given in one of the reports of the Franklin Home at Philadelphia. From it, it appears that, of 383 patients treated during the year, 331 were discharged. Of these, 139 were looked upon as permanently cured; men who showed some change (benefited only), 42; doubtful, 37; failures, 104; unknown, 9. 52 patients were still being treated at the end of the year.

In an interesting table of the condition of the patients, we find, under the denomination of married, 190; single, 120; widowers, 28; divorced, 18; separated, 27. From this, it is evident that matrimony is not all bliss, and we find, on going into the history of like cases, that the married contingent always heads the list. Taking the single, separated, and divorced cases together in the above table, they hardly equal those of the Benedicks. At the New York Christian

Home, since the opening of the institution, we discover, amongst a host of others that have been treated there, the following: lawyers, 190; journalists, 65; clergy, 20; naval officers, 14; physicians, 92; merchants, 242; Roman Catholic priests, 9. During 1890-91 there were treated at the Washingtonian Home, Boston, in the classes division: merchants, 188; lawyers, 16; physicians, 34; other professions, 103. The House of Correction, Philadelphia, affords records of 2,215 cases treated during the last seven years. The cases of delirium tremens numbered 122. I will now proceed to deal with the forms of disease as established and received by physicians with special experience in the treatment of alcoholism and insanity.

INHERITED FORM.

No sadder legacy can be left to a human being than the inherited disease of alcoholism. Insanity in any form is a deplorable thing, but no phase of mental breakdown is more far-reaching in its influence than that before us.

To Magnus Huss is due the honour of having been the first qualified observer who identified alcoholism as a diseased condition. Soon he was followed by Morrell, who very ably demonstrated the effects of the same upon the progeny of drunkards. A host of writers have since dealt with this form of disease, and have proved beyond cavil that inebriety may be handed down through successive generations. In 'Das Unbewusste,' the author advances a splendid definition of that quality known as instinct. He writes: 'In this sense it may be said that every instinct is in the last instance by its origin an acquired habit, and the proverb that "Habit is second nature" thus receives the unexpected supplement that habit is also the beginning and origin of the first nature, *i.e.*, of instinct. For it is always habit, *i.e.*, the frequent repetition of the same function, which so firmly impresses the mode of action, however acquired, upon the cerebral organs of the nervous system, that the predisposition becomes transmissible.' Lamarck defined instinct in a similar way. For the purpose of illustration, no better argument than the foregoing can be offered to establish an easy comprehension of how simple it is for a physical or material quality to be transmitted, allowing that traits of character and mind, being purely immaterial, are capable of transference. In fact, the offspring tend to inherit every attribute of the parents, mental or physical, material or immaterial; and, more remarkable still, this inheritance may remain latent for many years in the recipient and then appear with great force. Le Compte's family presented a startling proof of this. Blindness was inherited and transmitted through three generations, and nearly thirty children and grand-children were all affected at a corresponding age.

Gall has given a description of a Russian family, from which we learn that father and son died at au early age from alcoholic intoxication. The third generation was represented by a little boy, who on reaching the age of five years manifested an unquenchable craving for strong drink. Landor Gray, of New York, has related a remarkable instance of three generations, namely, father, son, and grandson, who on attaining the age of forty, developed similar symptoms of disease (alcoholic), with fatal results in two instances; at the present time the grandson is under treatment. In speaking of this form of drunkenness, Dr. Tuke, in his work on Insanity, says: 'This is a form of mental disorder which in an especial manner requires to be discriminated from what may be termed a merely physiological condition, in which the human animal chooses to indulge in alcoholic beverages to excess. On the one hand, the admission of this disease into the department of mental pathology does not need to make us conclude that there is no such thing as intemperance without disease; and on the other, the fact that the abuse of alcoholic drinks has oftentimes no disease to plead in its excuse, must not lead us to the opposite extreme of denying that a truly diseased cerebral condition may exist, the result of which is inebriety.' It is not difficult to understand that diseased organizations, no matter from what cause or kind of disease, may produce successors, whose discounted vitality, added to structural changes, are the factors in the ignition of some form of neurosis of a more or less pronounced type. It is almost impossible to get away from the striking evidence on this score. De Bouzareingue knew of a family in which the taint of alcoholism was transmitted, remarkable to say, from mother to daughter, and for many generations only on the female side. Persons of weakened intellect, having an hereditary taint, are more disposed to the crave for liquor, and have a tendency to become confirmed alcoholists. Grenier's studies led him to believe that this was the case. Piorry has written of a family in which every member became insane at forty. A telling illustration of the power of transmission is given by

Esquirol, in which three generations, father, son, and grandson, upon arriving at the fiftieth year, committed suicide.

I am acquainted with a family in Australia in which the desire for drink has been transmitted from the mother, a lady in a high social position, and very wealthy, to both her daughters. The father is a man highly esteemed, and enjoys, apart from his domestic trials, the most perfect health. In another case a lady, married, young, pretty, and the mother of several beautiful children, literally becomes insane two or three times a year from the drinking of spirits. Here the family history reveals transmission of the neurosis from the father. An able physician, an alienist, last year committed suicide in one of the colonies after a course of drinking. He had developed the morphine habit as well. In his case the heredity was traced to his mother. A remarkable instance of hereditary transmission was related to me during a visit to Washington in January, by Dr. Hammond, Surgeon-General, U.S.A. (retired). He stated : 'A gentleman informed me that his grandfather had become accustomed to wake up from sound sleep at twelve o'clock every night and drink a cup of tea, after which he would lie down and sleep quietly till morning. The father of my informant was a posthumous son, and his mother died in childbirth with him. He was English, and at an early age went to India with an uncle. One night, when he was about twenty years of age, he awoke suddenly with an intense desire for a cup of tea. He endeavoured to overcome the longing, but finally, being unable to sleep, got up, and, proceeding to an adjoining room, made himself a cup of tea, and then, going back to bed, soon fell asleep. He did not mention the circumstance at that time; in fact, it made no strong impression on his mind; but the next night the awaking, the desire, and the tea-making were repeated. At breakfast the following morning he alluded to the fact that he had twice been obliged to rise in the middle of the night and make himself a cup of tea, and laughingly suggested that perhaps it would be as well for him in future to have the materials in his bedroom. His uncle listened attentively, and, when the recital was finished, said:

'" Yes, have everything ready, for you will want your tea every night; your father took it at midnight for over twenty years, and you are like him in everything."

'The uncle was right; the midnight tea-drinking became a settled habit. Several years afterwards the gentleman returned to England, and there married. Of this marriage a son—my informant—was born, and six years subsequently the father died. The boy was sent to school till he was sixteen years old, when he was sent to Amsterdam as a clerk in the counting-house of his mother's brother, a banker of that city. He was kept pretty actively at work, and one night in particular did not get to bed till after twelve o'clock. Just as he was about to lie down, the idea struck him that a cup of tea would be a good thing. All the servants had retired, so the only thing to do was to make it himself. He did so, and then went to bed. The next night he again had his tea, and after that took it regularly, waking from sleep punctually for that purpose at twelve o'clock. Up to that time he had never been a tea-drinker, though he had occasionally tasted tea. Writing home to his mother, he informed her that he had taken to the custom of drinking tea, but had acquired the habit of taking it at a very inconvenient hour—twelve o'clock at night. She replied, telling him that he had come honestly by his liking, for his father and grandfather had had exactly the same habit. Previous to the reception of this letter he had never heard of the peculiarity of his father and grandfather.'

There is no escape from this singular evidence as to heredity being causative of mental conditions not incompatible with health. On the other hand, there are a vast number of instances in which transmissibility of neuroses is entirely absent. Again, in a family some members may seem to be healthy in every way; and, on the other hand, most pronounced mania may be developed by the others. Compensation for the non-exhibition of mental changes is often seen in the degeneration of the special organs of the body—as the lungs, liver, or kidneys. And diseases of any of these parts may come to light should the vitality of the person affected become lowered in any way from overwork, improper nourishment, defective hygienic surroundings, or other causes.

There is little doubt but that transmitted mental and physical imperfections may be manifested in various ways without minimising very seriously any special talent or faculty. And it is not difficult to understand how a person having a neurotic tendency may exhibit eccentricities which call forth ridicule and condemnation. Are the vagaries of genius to be explained in this way? Should insane symptoms appearing in such people surprise us? Remarkable advance or development of extraordinary or brilliant mental characteristics does not altogether depend upon mere intellectual cultivation. There is a stratum, inherent it may be called, in certain organizations which demands and attracts attention. Heredity is at the bottom of it all. Interchangeability of transmissible influences is, in our present knowledge, in an embryonic state of study, and should afford a fertile opportunity to the investigator of psychological problems and data. Déjerine looks upon heredity as a matter of the most vital importance in mental changes, and is inclined to think that in successive generations the same pathological mental states may be evinced, and that, unless great care is taken, the nervous organization may become more seriously affected from generation to generation. This might be set down as a process of degenerative heredity. The late Professor R. Demme, of Berne, considers that the alcoholic habit in parents is simply the expression of an inheritable psychopathic diathesis, showing itself in the following generation either as alcoholism or some other kind of specific psychosis. Barr has shown that in some of the more bibulous parts of Germany (called the drinking regions) the military draft is much smaller than in the more temperate localities. In Sweden, since the full effects of the Acts passed against drunkenness have been felt, Gyllenskiöld states that the number of debilitated men who were not equal to military service on account of their diminutive size and poor physique has diminished perceptibly.

The Medico-Psychological Society of France recently offered a prize for the ablest essay on the 'Influence of Heredity in Alcoholism.' The successful essayist was M. Paul Sollier. Very completely he has laid down the following classification: 'First, Dipsomaniacs (hereditary drunkards, who are not always intoxicated); secondly, Acquired Drunkards (non-hereditary, who are always intoxicated); thirdly, Hereditary Drunkards (who are always intoxicated).' Alcohol, on his showing, is more baneful to the hereditary class than to those of the acquired order. He cites hosts of cases to give force to this argument. A clever thesis by Le Grain resolves itself into the formulating of two propositions as follow: ' 1. Cerebral inferiority — the direct cause of the excesses in strong drink—has its origin most frequently in heredity; that is, excessive drinkers are degenerates. 2. Alcoholism is one of the most powerful causes of mental degeneration; that is, the sons of inebriates are degenerates. The relations between alcoholism and mental degeneration are comprised within this terribly vicious circle, which is irrefutably traced out and confirmed by innumerable most eloquent medical observations.' Heredity as a causation is estimated to be present in nearly 60 per cent. of all cases of chronic alcoholism. Injuries, railway shock, wasting diseases, are credited with producing 20 per cent. of the cases. Nervous exhaustion may account for another 10 per cent. Five per cent. can be laid to insanitary conditions and poor food. To unascertained causes a small percentage may be ascribed.

ACQUIRED FORM.

The Arabian physicians are responsible for the introduction of alcohol, but in doing so, they were careful enough to exercise a certain prudence in its use. It remained for a distinguished physician living in the fourteenth century, Arnold Villanova, to introduce it indiscriminately in the treatment of his cases. What had been a remedy soon became a luxury, and to many a necessity. Temperament has doubtless much to do with acquiring the alcohol habit. Let us first take that of the nervous order. How prone to the creation of an overdraft on the vitality is the possessor of a highly-constituted nervous organism, and what a sequence in the shape of depression of the most pronounced kind is the result! How unkind it appears to suggest to such sufferers that rest will soon set them right, and to tell them not to worry over matters! One could as easily stop an affrighted animal that has bolted as reason with the victim of a temporarily devitalized and exhausted nervous system. The very condition negatives treatment in the way of well-intended practical speeches, and these are precisely the cases that fly to some form of nerve-paralyzer with the object of relaxing the great tension under which they suffer. The phlegmatic temperament is not so apt to run down in the same way, and rarely seeks oblivion for the reason that stimulates that of the nervous form. If anything, it is from the fact that certain forms of liquor are pleasant as a beverage that causes the latter class to be consumers of the same, and not for the intoxicant effects, or slightly so. It cannot be denied that a subtle fascination is found in alcoholic liquor by vast numbers of people after an introduction to it has been established. Plautus says, *Ubi mel, ibi apes*. And to many people the simile of the bees and the honey applies forcibly. Like habits of morphinism, cocainism, and the use of chloral, the acquirement of that of alcoholism is easy, but extremely hard to relinquish. Alcohol, withal, is not to be condemned because its misuse entails danger to a few. As a remedy in certain conditions it is a most powerful aid, and such it will continue to be where its application is judiciously directed. Mental trouble, over-work, exhaustion of any kind, debility from ill-health, starvation, on the one hand, and occasions of festivity, merry-making of all kinds, social hospitality, and even funerals, on the other, are made the occasion and the excuse for indulgence in alcohol in some form or other! In fact, it is looked upon as a panacea for most ills. There are many good and generous people who do inestimable injury by pressing the use of liquors upon their friends. This is done with all good-nature and kindliness, but is most unjust to numbers of men and women whose moral courage may be terribly tried by placing them in the awkward position of saying 'No' on such occasions. A better understanding of the fact that a latent disease may be called into existence by demanding the acceptance of a special wine or liqueur on the part of a guest may tend to the non-compulsory system of drinking being adopted. There are thousands who would never touch alcoholic preparations were it not out of compliment to the host or hostess. Mistaken generosity of such a character only requires indication of its perilousness to ensure a release from a great social tyranny. The late Sir William Gull wrote: 'I think that instead of flying to alcohol, as some people do when they are exhausted, they might very well take to food, and would be very much better without the alcohol. If I am fatigued with over-work personally, my food is very simple; I eat the raisins instead of drinking the wine. I have had a very large experience in that practice for thirty years. This is my own personal experience, and I believe it is a very good and true experience. I should join issue at once with those who believe that intellectual work cannot be so well done without wine or alcohol; I should deny that proposition and hold to the very opposite. There is a great deal of injury done to health by the habitual use of wines in their various kinds, and alcohol in its various shapes, even in so-called moderate quantities. It leads to the degeneration of the tissues; it spoils the health and spoils the intellect.'

That indolence, want of occupation, a luxurious mode of living without sufficient exercise, prompts to the acquirement of habits of intemperance is exemplified very freely on all sides. Again, poverty, want of food, improper clothing, and conditions of life which may be designated homeless, tempt strongly to the relief of such unhappy circumstances by an indulgence in intoxicants. If excuse exists for either class, surely the latter merits our consideration. It appears to be a law of activities that an over-plus of nervous energy looks for explosion or an outlet, which seems to be necessary and natural to some persons, and very often takes the form of a 'spree' or course of alcoholic stimulants. The rationale of such a departure is difficult to arrive at.

Dr. R. Bird, formerly of the East Indian Army, has pointed out that perverted nutrition is often the cause of a morbid desire, and illustrates this by relating two cases that were under his care. 'The first was "E. B.," the wife of a river steamboat captain. Her husband told me "she drank like a fish," and had been drinking so for years. She drank anything she could get, and when ordinary drink was not forthcoming she would drink eau de Cologne, purchased from Hindoo pedlars. As she also suffered from rheumatism of the womb and copious leucorrhœa, I had her removed to hospital for treatment. Cure of the womb affection in a great degree cured the drink craving also, but not quite. Oxide of zinc, as recommended by Marcel, of Paris, and wild-thyme, as recommended by Salvatori, combined with seclusion in an institution where she acted as sewing mistress, were required to complete the cure of this. She ultimately returned to her husband reformed and thoroughly restored, nor did she in the subsequent years relapse, so far as I know. The other case was that of "M. W.," who, when I first came to know her, was the mother of eight children. In her last confinement she lost a great deal of blood, and subsequently developed a mad wish for liquor, to the great grief of her husband, a steady mechanic. It turned out, on inquiry, that she had for years previously been in the habit of starving both herself and her children for purposes of economy. Iron, good food, and change to a more temperate climate in this case cured the anæmia and drink craving too.'

It is a common thing in Great Britain to give stimulants, particularly gin, to women during pregnancy, and following the birth of the child, which is a most pernicious habit. Latterly it has been suspected that a number of cases of primary internal cancer are due to brandy, whisky, and gin nipping. Alluding to moderate drinking, Dr. Harley writes : 'The effects of moderate drinking manifest themselves in such a variety of different forms, that even when their true nature is recognised, the general practitioner has not the opportunity of seeing a sufficient number of any one of them to admit of his drawing conclusions from them.' Further, 'the men who have most experience of the severer forms of disease directly traceable to the effects of moderate drinking are, in general, merely those who, like myself, made liver and kidney diseases a special study.' In the United States the life assurance offices have issued instructions to the medical examiners as to what is termed drawing the line in cases of moderate drinking. An illustration of the regulation laid down is given in the daily allowance made under what is called Anstie's limit, which, it must be confessed, is not a very niggardly affair after all. According to Anstie, the quantity is 'equivalent to one and a half ounces of absolute alcohol; three ounces of ardent spirits; two wineglasses of port; one pint bottle of claret, champagne, or other light wine; three tumblerfuls of ale or porter; four or five tumblerfuls of ale or light beer.' According to the calculations made by the life offices, risk only occurs to health should the amount given above be exceeded. That numbers of persons are benefited by the exhibition, under certain conditions and restrictions, of some form of alcohol is demonstrable beyond question. In small quantities it is found useful in aiding digestion, and, although not a food, its advantages are direct in promoting the assimilation of other and more nutritive materials. It must not be imagined for one moment that alcohol in any shape should be ordered for a person with an hereditary or neurotic predisposition. In speaking of its use medicinally, this must at all times be understood.

Sir Henry Thompson, in a letter to the Archbishop of Canterbury, says: 'I have long had the conviction that there is no greater cause of evil, moral and physical, in this country than the use of alcoholic beverages. I do not mean by this that extreme indulgence which produces drunkenness. The habitual use of fermented liquors to an extent far short of what is necessary to produce that condition, and such as is quite common in all ranks of society, injures the body and diminishes the mental power to an extent which I think few people are aware of. Such, at all events, is the result of observation during more than twenty years of professional life devoted to hospital practice, and to private, in every rank above it. Thus I have no hesitation in attributing a very large proportion of some of the most dangerous and painful maladies which come under my notice, as well as those which every medical man has to treat, to the ordinary and daily use of fermented drink taken in the quantity which is conventionally deemed moderate. Whatever may be said in regard to its evil influence on the mental and moral faculties, as to the fact stated above I feel that I have a right to speak with authority; and I do so solely because it appears to me a duty, especially at this moment, not to be silent on a matter of such extreme importance. I know full well how unpalatable is such truth, and how such a declaration brings me into a painful conflict—I had almost said with a national sentiment—with the time-honoured and prescriptive usages of our race.'

In concluding my remarks upon this form of

alcoholism, the treatment of which, together with those of the inherited and infantile forms, I propose to deal with in a special chapter, I do not know of a better exposition of the baneful effects of alcohol used in an incautious way in the sick-room than that given by Dr. Harley, F.R.S., and also his summary as to the therapeutical advantages of alcoholic stimulants. He writes :

'This part of my subject I must premise by remarking that, from it so happening that in certain cases of disease alcohol is tolerated by weak patients to a surprising extent, many of us have fallen into the error of thinking that in all forms of exhausting disease an equal amount of toleration to alcoholic stimulants exists. Personal observation has, however, opened my eyes to the fact that, so far from this being the case, in many, I think I might even go so far as to say in most, cases of disease exactly the reverse is the fact. For I have repeatedly come across patients, weakened by disease, who have exhibited marked sensibility to the intoxicating effects of alcoholic stimulants, and to whom they have appeared to me to be an actual bane.

'As illustrative examples are invariably the most convincing forms of argument, instead of dealing in generalities, I shall cite specific cases. As, however, the gentlemen in whose practices they occurred are still alive, and will have no difficulty in recognising their own cases, for obvious reasons I must avoid mentioning either names, localities, or dates. By so doing, while the value of the inference to be drawn from them will not be diminished, all risk of giving offence will be avoided.

'The first case I shall refer to will be one of severe typhoid fever, of a low asthenic type, that being the form of disease in which the most marked benefits are said to be derived from the free use of alcoholic stimulants. The patient was a member of our own profession, and was attended by two of his personal friends, the one an able general practitioner, the other a physician to one of our metropolitan hospitals. When I was asked to see the case, I was told (if I remember rightly, for I am at present writing from memory) that it was the nineteenth day of the disease. On reaching the bedside I received a shock, for when I had last seen the patient, only a month before, he was the very picture of health. Now he lay in a helpless and prostrate state of coma, with congested eyes, flushed face, and a clammy, disagreeable smelling skin. To rouse him to consciousness was impossible, even so far as to get him to protrude his tongue. The other signs and symptoms, being merely those of ordinary severe typhoid, need not be referred to. All that I require to add is that the man seemed on the brink of the tomb. Twenty-four hours at most would apparently suffice to see him a corpse. Having satisfied myself as to the patient's state, we retired to the dressing-room, and no sooner was the door shut than I emphatically said to my two co-consultants, "I don't think that this profound coma can possibly be due entirely to the disease. His breath smells so strongly of brandy that I think it is in great measure the result of the alcohol. Were I you, I would stop the brandy entirely and give him milk and warm tea in its stead, and probably the coma will disappear." The hint was taken and acted upon, and when we met twenty-four hours later we had the pleasure of finding the patient able to answer questions quite coherently, though only monosyllabically. As the patient's state of prostration was extreme, the brandy was resumed, but now in only one-sixth the quantity, and in merely teaspoonfuls at a time, instead of in half-ounces as before, being only given along with beef-tea, milk, or some other kind of easily assimilated liquid food.

'This was a most instructive case in more ways than one; for, among other things, there was not only twice a most dangerous relapse before convalescence was established, but the patient's whole body, for four or five consecutive days, was covered with large raised purpuric blotches, exactly as if the case had been one of purpura hæmorrhagica. And I could not help thinking that the appearing of the blotches in such a form was in some measure due to his system having been for several days poisonously saturated with alcohol. Be that as it may, the other portions of this brief report will, I think, suffice to show that even the ablest amongst us is liable to fall into the error of giving a weak patient too much stimulant. Had this man died in his comatose state, instead of recovering, the severity of the disease would have been alone blamed for it, and the brandy have altogether escaped censure.

'The next case I will refer to is of a very different character, seeing that it was one in which both doctor and patient (?) were hoodwinked by the combined action of nurse and maid. The patient was a well-developed buxom widow of some three-and-thirty summers, and when I was asked to see her, I was informed that she had been subject to severe neuralgic headaches, with partial loss of consciousness, ever since she had had a backward fall from the step of a carriage, some fifteen months previously. The immediate result of the fall had been an attack of spinal paralysis, which necessitated her lying in a supine position during eight months. The cause of my being then consulted, however, was the supposed supervention of an attack of insanity, which was causing great uneasiness to the family, as her father had died an imbecile, from softening of the brain. On being ushered into the bedroom, I found it darkened, and, in reply to my inquiry why it was so, I was told that it was on account of the patient always seeing a big black cat on the top of the wardrobe when the room was illuminated. Knowing that, if this delusion was the offspring of brain disease, it was just as likely that the black cat would be seen in the darkened as in the lighted room, I ordered the window-curtains to be withdrawn. No sooner was this done than I noticed a champagne and a brandy bottle on the washstand, and, when I stooped over the patient to examine her pupils, I perceived that the breath was strongly impregnated with the odour of brandy, while at the same time she replied in such a rambling manner to my questions as to leave no doubt upon my mind that she was under the influence of alcohol. Notwithstanding that, I was solemnly assured by the nurse, as well as by the maid, that no stimulants, "except a very little wine," had been given to her. The sequel is soon told. Nurse and maid were firmly admonished not to give her one drop more of any kind of stimulant. A blister, which had been applied shortly before my arrival, was ordered to be removed from the nape of the neck, an ice-bag to be placed upon the forehead, and milk, with soda-water, and beef-tea substituted for all other kinds of nutriment. This change in the treatment soon bore its fruits. On seeing the patient in the following afternoon, a marked amelioration was found to have taken place. The black cat, as well as the restlessness of manner and incoherent talking, had disappeared, and a few days sufficed to remove the headache. Seven years have passed since then, and although the patient has had several attacks of severe neuralgia in the interval, never again has she been troubled with black cats or any other kind of mental hallucination. This fact I learned from herself a few weeks ago, when she happened to come into my study along with another patient, an intimate friend of hers. So the conclusion I have arrived at is, that the appearance of the black cat, as well as of the delirium, was more due to the excessive use of stimulants in a weak-headed individual than to the existence of any hereditary cerebral disease.

'The third and last illustration of the baneful effects which sometimes accrue from the injudicious employment of alcohol in the sick-room is one which shows the dangers which may arise from giving a nurse a discretionary power in their administration.

'Along with an operative surgeon I was in attendance upon a schoolboy, aged fifteen, suffering from acute and severe tonsillitis. Both tonsils were incised with great relief to the distressed breathing—I should rather say, impending suffocation—and on the following morning, although the patient was greatly exhausted from four or five days' extreme suffering, and total inability to swallow food, I considered him out of danger.

'It so happened that on the morning in question my colleague was unable to keep his appointment, and made his visit an hour later. Finding, as I had done, that a great improvement had taken place, and thinking that stimulants might now be employed with advantage, he told the nurse to give the boy half an ounce of brandy as often as she thought fit. She accordingly did so, and began giving him a tablespoonful half-hourly. After the fifth or sixth dose the boy began tossing himself about in bed, and talking incoerently. The nurse having heard of the delirium of exhaustion, and that the free administration of stimulants was the best way to treat it, immediately jumped to the conclusion that this was a case of the kind, and that the more brandy she gave the better it would be for the patient. Accordingly she began giving it every quarter of an hour. He rapidly, however, got more and more delirious, and I was hastily sent for, the messenger stating that the boy was raving, and they could not keep him in bed. On reaching the room, I found the patient tossing himself about like a drunken person, and singing as loudly as the state of his throat would permit. The delirium seemed to be nothing whatever but the delirium of intoxication. And a few questions quickly set my mind at rest on this point. For I learned that the boy, who had probably never in his life before tasted brandy, with a constitution weakened by disease and want of food, had within six hours had certainly had not less than ten ounces of brandy administered to him, the nurse remarking that "as he was so very bad she had given him half a wine-glassful just before my arrival, but it had done him no good."

'The stimulants were ordered to be discontinued, and hot tea to be given instead, with the view of counteracting the deleterious action of the alcohol on the nervous system. The mischief had, however, already been done, for the boy rapidly sank into a state of insensibility, and died without regaining consciousness. The result of this case taught me the lesson never to authorize a nurse, be her training what it might, nor the friends of a patient, be their education what it may, to administer stimulants at discretion; but invariably to specify a definite quantity beyond which they are not to proceed except under medical instruction.

'These three cases being sufficient of themselves to exhibit my views of the baneful effects which occasionally spring from the injudicious employment of alcohol in the sick-chamber, I now pass on to the consideration of the beneficial results which may accrue from its administration. The following are its therapeutic effects:

'*Firstly*.—Having already said that the primary effect of alcohol is to stimulate the heart's action, I now add that I consider it one of the most valuable agents in the Pharmacopœia in cases of cardiac syncope, from its not only increasing the heart's action, but at the same time possessing the additional advantage of indirectly stimulating the brain by increasing the flow of blood through the cerebral vessels.

'*Secondly*.—Alcohol taken into the stomach acts potently as an antiflatulent (in cases of disengagement of gas on account of stomachal fermentation) from its possessing not only the power of arresting fermentation, by virtue of its antiseptic properties, but likewise of stimulating the stomach to contraction, and thereby causing it to expel the already generated gas by eructations.

'*Thirdly*.—Alcohol acts as a diaphoretic, by accelerating the circulation and dilating the cutaneous capillaries, especially when it is given along with hot water.

'*Fourthly*.— Alcohol possesses to some extent diuretic properties, for it increases the urinary secretion, more particularly when it is combined with certain volatile empyreumatic substances, as in the form of gin, and some kinds of beer.

'*Fifthly*.—Alcohol, when taken diluted with hot water, has emmenagogue properties, probably by not only increasing the circulation in the uterus, but at the same time dilating its bloodvessels.

'*Sixthly*.—Alcohol has a perfect right to be denominated an antispasmodic, for it has the power, by virtue of its paralyzing properties, of relaxing muscular spasm.

'*Seventhly*.—Alcohol may be employed in certain cases as an antipyretic, for after its primary stimulating effects have passed off, and been succeeded by its depressing action, it materially lowers bodily temperature.

'*Eighthly*.—Alcohol is in some forms of disease a useful soporific, for although its action in this respect is most probably due to the same cause as opium, it can be given in cases where opium is counter-indicated, as, for example, in certain forms of liver disease. For it neither arrests the biliary secretion and gives rise to white stools, as opium often does, nor increases the tendency to constipation. The employment of alcohol as a soporific in liver cases, however, requires very careful handling.

'*Ninthly.*—Alcohol in large doses is a powerful anæsthetic. No one can doubt this who has ever noticed the trifling effects blows and bruises have on the dormant sensibility of a drunken man.

'*Tenthly.*—Alcohol is an undoubted narcotic. The combined words " dead drunk " sufficiently testify this fact.'

INFANTILE FORM.

It is inexplicable for what reason or reasons parents, guardians, and friends dose innocent little children with wines, beers, or other beverages possessing certain percentages of alcohol. Want of reflection and ignorance as to the possible injury being done explain the action of some people; but there is no doubt in a vast number of instances the administration is due to gross carelessness and want of consideration for the future of the unfortunate child or children. The child of neurotic parents, where an insane or alcoholic taint is declared, we frequently find to be precocious in many ways. This is a state of things that requires sedative regimen, in the way of avoidance of all recognition of the unusual qualities displayed. But such, unfortunately, is not the way children of the description mentioned are treated. Every possible means of leading them on to an exhibition of their all-too-early powers (addressing them in language only suited to educated adults) is a stimulus to the brain, and at what cost! Very proud are the fond, but extremely foolish, parents of the versatility displayed, forgetting that the nervous organization of the child is only in an embryonic stage, and that the physique of the victim of parental vanity and self-congratulation is immature. If the morning of life to the child be bright and happy, the afternoon and evening of its career display and bring into relief a stunted and debilitated subject of early forcing (grafted upon a stem of hereditary neuroses), and a weakened mental balance. How easy is it in such a case to develop a tendency towards a craving for relief from an overwrought and crushed nervous system! These are the children to whom wine is frequently given, under the impression that their singular ability requires special consideration.

Dr. Crothers, amongst other cases, speaks of one in which a physician had given tincture of cinchona to a neurotic infant one year of age. In a little time the child cried for the medicine, and nothing would pacify it until it was given. The tonic was changed, but the child was satisfied with nothing but the tincture. On investigation, it was found that the baby had an alcoholic mother, who died soon after its birth—an illustration of early manifested heredity. In a second case, an infant of two months old could only be reduced to tranquillity by a few drops of spirits. On the appearance of the person who gave the spirits it would stop nursing, and cry until the alcohol had been administered.

In the Children's Hospital at Berne undoubted cases of heredity amongst the inmates are seen, showing itself in the form of an almost unquenchable thirst at intervals.

Hitzig asserts that the offspring of alcoholists suffer the inheritance of an equal, if not greater, tendency to disorders and diseases of the nervous organization than children born of nervous or insane parents. We see evidence of this around us at all times, in the deaths from convulsions and allied troubles.

Dr. A. W. Edis says that 'the premature deaths of the 130,000 children dying in England in 1876 before attaining the age of one year were due in great measure to the ignorance of the mothers in giving wrong food, and to the pernicious delusion of nursing mothers that they require to be kept up by alcoholic liquors.' This is a strong indictment against parents; and still the death-rate is kept up. The children that escape, and reach early adult life, frequently exhibit symptoms of an insane or criminal type; and where there has been a great drain on the system, a mania for drink may be found.

Dr. R. Bird, who has already been quoted, published, amongst other cases, the following : 'Case I.—J. H., an infant, while suffering from malarious diarrhœa, showed an abiding desire for gin and brandy. When she could get it she would drink as much as 10 or 12 oz. a day. This amount made her happy, but never very drunk. It was her chief sustenance for some months, and under its influence the diarrhœa got well. The craving for drink disappeared with the disease. When I last heard of her she was the sober mother of a family, living with her husband in a village near Newcastle, England.'

This is not an uncommon occurrence, parallels having been known in both the colonies and Great Britain.

In Case II., 'H. R., a scrofulous boy of two years,

while suffering from chronic dysentery, developed an insane appetite for brandy. When this was first offered to him he drank it greedily and screamed for more, and for weeks brandy was his cry, his joy, and his support. Ultimately he got rid of his dysentery and drink-craving altogether.'

That such a line of treatment was judicious or careful is open to question. No doubt Dr. Bird gauged his cases correctly and knew what he was doing. I doubt, however, if such a policy would be looked upon kindly by the profession of the present day, in the face of the knowledge of the dangers that might be apt to arise at a later period from a wholesale exhibition of alcohol, as carried out in the cases just noticed. To my mind, the absorption of a quantity of liquor containing alcohol, of either a high or low percentage, means simply nothing more nor less than the temporary, and perhaps permanent, strangling of the growing nervous matter, and a stamping out or modifying of the brain-cells, the healthy growth of which is so necessary in every way to the ultimate expansion of the intellect.

During a period of twelve years, Demme, of Berne, obtained accurate knowledge of the private circumstances of ten families, belonging on the one hand to the drinking, and on the other to the temperate, class. He writes: 'The direct posterity of ten families of drunkards, in which alcoholism of one parent or of both, or even of previous generations, is shown, amounted to fifty-seven children; but of these, twenty-five children died during the first weeks or months of life, part of them from lack of vitality, part through eclamptic seizures (œdema of the brain and its membranes). Six children were idiots; five children exhibited marked backwardness of growth in height, remaining almost dwarfish; five children, as they became older, were attacked with epilepsy; one boy was attacked with severe chorea, terminating finally in idiocy; five children had congenital diseases (chronic hydrocephalus, hare-lip, club-foot). What is especially interesting is, that two of the epileptics referred to were themselves given to the abuse of alcohol, as a result of hereditary transmission; the outbreak of their trouble was directly connected with most acute alcoholic intoxication, *i.e.*, was directly continuous with it. Thus, of fifty-seven children of drunkards, there were only ten, or 17·5 per cent., in a normal condition and with normal development of body and mind, at least during their childhood.

'Contrast this with observations upon the ten families free from all alcoholic influence and living very temperate lives, as far as alcoholic drinks were concerned. Only five out of their direct descendants of sixty-one children died from diseases connected with want of vitality, and four children suffered in later childhood with curable affections of the nervous system. Only two children showed congenital defects. The remaining fifty children (81·9 per cent.) of the temperate were normal in condition, and during childhood, at least, showed normal further development of physical and mental powers.'

It will be said that many children are accustomed to have spirits, wines, or other beverages given to them, and without evident harm. This will not be denied for a moment; but it will be found that the majority of such children rarely live beyond childhood. The amount of slaughter going on amongst young children from this cause is enormous; but the mortality is rarely laid at the proper door by the misguided, but in some instances negligent, parents. There is a class of women, erroneously styled nurses, who have had no training whatever beyond that handed down in a rule-of-thumb sort of manner, who are responsible for a deal of the infantile form of alcoholism. Custom or habit is a difficult thing to shake; but the custom of giving alcohol to infants of any age (unless under medical advice) is one that should be discontinued at once, without waiting for a suggestion of the kind from any quarter.

CHAPTER IV.

INSANITY AND ALCOHOLISM.

INSANITY is a term involving almost hopeless perplexity in deciding upon a definition that may convey and express in a sufficiently lucid manner or form that which can be easily understood and accepted. Speaking roughly, we may consider it as a general term, indicating a mental state opposed to sanity; sanity, as we understand it, being a condition or state of mind compatible with a proper performance and discharge of the duties which every man owes to his Creator, his fellow-beings, and himself. Where the power of inhibition (or self-control) is weakened or temporarily in abeyance, insanity is indicated by the disorder of conduct and the failure of adjustment of self to surroundings.

Let us for a moment realize what takes place upon the imbibition of alcohol. After absorption into the blood from the stomach, it is almost immediately brought into contact with the nervous matter, acting upon it powerfully. What is the sequence, supposing the intoxicant to be partaken of freely? Does the man conduct himself as ordinarily? Is he as guarded and tactful as is his wont? *In vino veritas.* Temporarily a man intoxicated is just as much insane as any inmate of a lunatic asylum. Singularly, where an inheritance of nervous instability is handed down, we do not find the manifestations common to drunkenness take the ordinary form—such as a difficulty in articulation, an awkwardness of carriage, and an uncertainty in using the hands. No; none of the muscular paralyses may be present; yet, on the other hand, there may be an exhibition of mania so violent and extreme as to necessitate detention as a lunatic, which the patient undoubtedly is. What do we find a day or two later? Simply that, on the elimination of the alcohol from the system, the man or woman becomes rational and sane. These are the cases that swell the ranks of murderers and other criminals. Another thing: their seeming coolness in the dock, placid, confident, is against them in the issue of the trial which means imprisonment or execution. A man who is suffering from delirium tremens may commit murder, and be quite safe as regards the law. Others, again, who from birth have carried about with them an hereditary tendency to the taking of alcohol, may, in a state of mania, execute a similar deed, and be convicted for the same. In drunkenness the brain appears to be affected much more in its middle and lower centres than in the higher. In chronic inflammation of the brain, which is the basis of general paralysis of the insane, the change may be induced by alcohol. In general paralysis, which may be set down as almost an exact counterpart of drunkenness, we sometimes find the movements abnormal, and the mental faculties clear or nearly so. Again, it is not uncommon to meet with cases in which the mind is altered, and the powers of co-ordination intact. Exaggeration in a morbid form of the tension of nervous energy is usually only discernible or found in cases of general paralysis of the insane and alcoholism. *Coup-de-soleil* predisposes to drink and insanity; also to the explosion of nerve-molecules on stimulation, as by alcohol. When we discern in a man who has been steadily drinking an alteration of habit of a striking character, as is evidenced by some disorder of conduct too patent to be overlooked, we may safely infer that mental alienation is taking place. Disorder of mind is bound to be present in such a case. A man may, however, have disorder of mind without insanity existing. What a man thinks or feels is difficult to estimate; how he acts is open to observation. Kolk, Niemeyer, and others speak of cases in which hallucinations were present, coexistent with local maladies. On the removal of the latter the mental symptoms cleared. And so it is with insanity the result of drink. Remove the one, and the mental condition under judicious treatment will, in many cases, be improved and perhaps cured. An alcoholist may not transmit the crave to the offspring, but it must not be forgotten that the inheritance may be an undue instability of the nervous organization, which may lead to some form of insanity or mental breakdown, if the subject is exposed to over-stimulation of any kind, or to the action of narcotics. Alcohol would, of course, be a rank poison. Recently the writer was called in consultation on a case in Melbourne. The patient had been drinking for years, and his family doctor looked upon treatment as useless. On examination the man was found to be in a state of insanity, and no doubt had been mad for years. He had threatened to murder some members of his family, and was known to be conducting his business in a strange way; otherwise, as it appeared, his friends would not have interfered with him. Very complete evidence is shown that a latency and reversion is sometimes illustrated in an extraordinary way; thus a generation may lose the neurotic or alcoholic taint; the same reappearing in the second or third generations in the form of insanity, epilepsy, or some other kind of brain degeneration or alteration. The neuroses appear to have remained latent and dormant. The insane asylums in Germany during one year received 1,614 patients suffering from mania due to intoxicants. In 1886, in the hospitals there, 1,213 men and 121 women died of delirium tremens. Amongst the prisoners in the German prisons convicted of murder 46 per cent. were known to have used liquor; and in going more closely into the matter, it was found that 41 per cent. were chronic drunkards. How many of these convicts may have been in an insane state? Sixty-three per cent. of those who committed manslaughter were found to be drinkers; assaults of a violent character were in 74 per cent. of the cases committed by drunkards; rape by 60 per cent.; and the percentage in other crimes varied from 40 to 80 per cent. Perjury alone showed the smallest percentage amongst habitual topers—viz., 26 per cent.

In Spain, according to Dr. Angel Pulido, the expense in connection with the maintenance of lunatics for the province of Madrid has risen from 50,000 pesetas in 1878-79 to over 200,000 pesetas in 1890-91. This increase in insanity is attributed largely to alcoholism.

CHAPTER V.

ALCOHOLIC TRANCE AND CRIME.

IT must be obvious to the veriest tyro in the laws of physiology that any agent which produces alteration in the tissue and matters of which the human body is composed, and where the changes that have taken place are in the direction of destruction or degeneration, must, as a matter of fact, diminish or put out of joint the normal functions. Where a man has absorbed nicotine, it is well known how much the heart becomes affected, leading to a host of alarming symptoms. The use of excessive doses of quinine has, at times, caused strange brain indications. Cocaine, so terribly seductive, from a state of melancholy and wretchedness plunges its victim into a condition of dreamy intoxication, a pleasure of a languorous nature, with phantasies as if listening to delicious and heavenly music. So its votaries say. But the cost very often is premature death. Why, with the remarkable affinity which alcohol is so well known to have for nervous matter, should it not be possible for vague psychic phenomena to be brought into play? So repeated is the statement made by prisoners when on trial for murder and other offences that they have no knowledge or memory of the act, that some form of investigation as to the surroundings of the delinquent at or about the time of the crime or crimes is surely demanded. In December, in San Francisco, I examined a man who had just returned to consciousness after remaining in a state of catalepsy for three days. The patient was found in his pyjamas running at full speed through the streets about one a.m., and taken to the hospital. Being aware of his tendency to trance, Mr. McIvor-Tyndal (the patient) always carries letters with him, as a protection, he puts it, against being buried alive. His family is highly neurotic on the maternal side. Tyndal has no recollection of what takes place in one of his nerve-storms.

The case of John B., aged forty-two, a partner in a mercantile house, single and a moderate wine-drinker, is extremely curious. He had never been intoxicated, but had suffered from severe headache after using wine freely. He spent the summer in Newport, and became acquainted with a French lady, whose company was agreeable. No intimacy or thought of marriage had occurred to him. One day he suffered more severely than ever from the effects of the wine taken the night before. Headache and profound muscular languor, with mental dulness, were present. He went over to the club and drank champagne, feeling much better. From this time his memory became confused. Two weeks later he recovered, and found that he had married this French lady and was on a bridal trip. He had no recollection of any event which had happened, nor could he recall in the slightest degree any event of the past. It was ascertained that he had drank steadily of champagne, and appeared particularly clear and bright, and thoroughly conscious of all his surroundings. The only unusual thing noticed was his inclination to fall asleep if the surroundings became monotonous and still. The second day of the trance he proposed marriage at the earliest possible moment. He called on a clergyman and arranged the time. A few friends were present, and nothing unusual was noticed in his manner or conversation. After the marriage they went by short journeys to Boston, Portland, Montreal, and Saratoga, where he awoke. In the meantime he drank champagne regularly and seemed cheerful and happy. He applied for a divorce, and alleged that he was in a state of stupor, and did not comprehend what he had done. This was denied by the court, after which a mutual settlement was agreed upon. The clergyman and other friends noted that he drank more than usual, and seemed under the influence of spirits, but acted rationally, and was apparently conscious of all his acts. Some of his friends were sceptical of his alleged amnesia, or trance condition. One year later, while travelling for the firm on business, he suddenly took a steamer for Liverpool, and awoke at sea without the slightest idea of any plan or possible motive. He remembered having drank freely with a friend at Boston, and retired to the hotel. It appears the next morning after paying his bill he drove to the steamer, bought a round trip, and after wandering around went to his state-room and remained until he awoke four days later. Evidently this is a typical case of trance that is growing worse, and unless he abstains absolutely from spirits, and has exact medical treatment, the future will be doubtful.

Somnambulism is a form of trance, exemplifications

of which are frequently found in the practice of British practitioners. In this state the subject can be directed to perform most of the acts common to a person when awake. In 'La Sonnambula' a good illustration of this is given. Epilepsy and chronic alcoholism are the factors that contribute the largest quota of cases showing blanks of memory and definite periods of loss of consciousness; while concurrently the subjects of the same conduct the affairs of life in an automatic manner not always recognisable by their friends. Later on many of the actions performed during this state of trance are denied, on the grounds of no memory or knowledge of the same. This trance-like condition may exist for days together. In the face of strong circumstantial evidence it is a puzzle to all classes of men to find a prisoner denying in the most placid manner all recollection of the deed. If his rebuttal is true, two known conditions can be offered or suggested to explain his *lapsus memoriæ*. The prisoner may have been a pronounced alcoholist or an epileptic. A trance-state might be due to other than these causes, but information and evidence are wanting as to the conditions necessary to occasion it. Pathologically speaking, a basis for the trance-state is made out where epilepsy has been proved and known to exist. Insanity has produced cataleptic phenomena and trance symptoms. *Coup-de-soleil* and heat apoplexy have been responsible for like nervous displays. Only recently, at an inquest on a former staff-sergeant in the British army, it was stated in evidence that the man had suffered from a sunstroke some few years back in India. Later on he took to drink, and finally ended his life by taking poison. The jury very intelligently brought in a verdict of 'Suicide while of unsound mind, induced by intemperance,' overlooking entirely the real cause of the man's brain change, viz., the *coup-de-soleil*. Again, at Eastbourne, in April, a man was charged with attempting to murder his son. The prisoner returned home under the influence of drink, and after questioning his three boys about twopence which was missing, said he would have the truth or kill all three. Subsequently he fired at one boy with a rifle, the bullet missing and lodging in the wall. The prisoner, in court, said he did not remember the occurrence. Here was a history of alcohol, mania, and crime—the man for a time being to all intents and purposes a lunatic. Had Deeming, in the murder trial recently completed at Melbourne, been able to substantiate his statements by independent witnesses, there was a chance of the proceedings terminating in a different way. He may have been one of those creatures known as moral paralytics, and, if his epilepsy was a real disease, it would have proved a difficult point for the prosecution to override. The man's career of robbery and murder, allied to motive and evidence of calculation, renders it difficult to believe that he was other than a cultivated slaughterer of his species. Added to this, he possessed a power of resource and a faculty for mendacity of a high order.

There is a phase about Deeming's conduct which at first sight might incline one to giving credence to the theory of insanity. His method of killing at Rainhill and Windsor pointed to a monomania for that sort of thing. That a mental haze of some peculiar nature surrounded the man, no psychologist would for one moment deny.

In the present state of the law, and the obscurity touching mental diseases, it is exceedingly difficult to know where to lessen or increase liability for offences. If crime is the outcome of degenerate progenitors, then indeed is the sin of the father visited upon the sons. To draw the line where crime ends and disease begins involves a stupendous task for a commission of legal and medical experts. What ingenuity and forensic skill will have to be exercised in fixing the standard of recognised mental diseases from any and every cause, defining grades of criminality or exemption! The project, if ever undertaken, will savour of a Utopian character. Common-sense will determine what is to be done, outside of all specializing on the part of alienists or the technicalities of legal *dicta*.

The following cases and remarks by Dr. T. D. Crothers are given to emphasise some of the points we have been considering, which serve to support the assertion of no memory of the act or crime with which they are charged, so often made by prisoners in court:

HORSE-STEALING.

The first case is that of A., who was repeatedly arrested for horse-stealing, and always claimed to be unconscious of the act. This defence was regarded with ridicule by the court and jury, and more severe sentences were imposed, until finally he died in prison. The evidence offered in different trials in defence was, that his father was weak-minded and died of consumption, and his mother was insane for many years and died in an asylum. His early life was one of hardship, irregular living, and no training. At sixteen he entered the army, and suffered from exposure, disease, and sunstroke, and began to drink spirits to excess at this time. At twenty he was employed as a hack-driver, and ten years later became owner of a livery stable. He drank to excess at intervals, yet during this time attended to business, acting sanely, and apparently conscious of all his acts, but often complained he could not recollect what he had done while drinking. When about thirty-four years of age he would, while drinking, drive strange horses to his stable, and claim that he had bought them. The next day he had no recollection of these events, and made efforts to find the owners of these horses and return them. It appeared that, while under the influence of spirits, the sight of a good horse, hitched up by the roadside alone, created an intense desire to possess and drive it. If driving his own horse, he would stop and place it in a stable, then go and take the new horse, and after a short drive put it up in his own stable, then go and get his own horse. The next day all this would be a blank, which he could never recall. On several occasions he displayed reasoning cunning, in not taking a horse when the owners or drivers were in sight. This desire to possess the horse seemed under control, but when no one was in sight all caution left him, and he displayed great boldness in driving about in the most public way. If the owner should appear and demand his property, he would give it up in a confused, abstracted way. No scolding or severe language made any impression on him. Often, if the horse seemed weary, he would place it in the nearest stable, with strict orders to give it special care. On one occasion he joined in a search of a stolen horse, and found it in a stable where he had placed it many days before. Of this he had no recollection. In another instance he sold a horse which he had taken, but did not take any money, making a condition that the buyer should return the horse if he did not like it. His horse-stealing was all of this general character. No motive was apparent, or effort at concealment, and, on recovering from his alcoholic excess, he made every effort to restore the property, expressing great regrets, and paying freely for all losses. The facts of these events fully sustained his assertion of unconsciousness, yet his apparent sanity was made the standard of his mental condition. The facts of his heredity, drinking, crime, and conduct all sustained his assertion of unconsciousness of these events. This was an alcoholic trance state, with kleptomaniac impulses.

WIFE MURDER.

The next case was that of B., who was executed for the murder of his wife. He asserted positively that he had no memory or consciousness of the act, or any event before or after. The evidence indicated that he was an inebriate of ten years' duration, dating from a sunstroke. He drank periodically, for a week or ten days at a time, and during this period was intensely excitable and active. He seemed always sane and conscious of his acts and surroundings, although intensely suspicious, exacting, and very irritable to all his associates. When sober he was kind, generous, and confiding, and never angry or irritable. He denied all memory of his acts during this period. While his temper, emotions, and conduct were greatly changed during this time, his intellect seemed more acute and sensitive to all his acts and surroundings. His business was conducted with usual skill, but he seemed unable to carry out any oral promises, claiming he could not recollect them. His business associates always put all bargains and agreements in writing when he was drinking, for the reason he denied them when sober. But when not drinking, his word and promise was always literally carried out. He broke up the furniture of his parlour when in this state, and injured a trusted friend, and in many ways showed violence from no cause or reason, and afterwards claimed no memory of it. After these attacks were over, he expressed great alarm and sought in every way to repair the injury. Finally, he struck his wife with a chair and killed her, and awoke the next day in gaol, and manifested the most profound sorrow. While he disclaimed all knowledge of the crime, he was anxious to die, and welcomed his execution. This case was a periodical inebriate with maniacal and homicidal tendencies. His changed conduct and unreasoning, motiveless acts pointed to a condition of trance. His assertion of no memory was sustained by his conduct after, and efforts to find out what he had done and repair the injury.

FORGERY.

The third case was that of C., a man of wealth and character, who forged a large note, drew the money, and went to a distant city on a visit. He was tried and sentenced to state prison. The defence was no memory or consciousness of the act by reason of excessive use of alcohol. This was treated with ridicule. Although he had drank to excess at the time of and before the crime, he seemed rational and acted in no way as if he did not understand what he was doing. Both his parents were neurotics, and he began to drink in early life, and for years was a moderate drinker. He was a successful manufacturer, and only drank to excess at times for the past five years. He complained of no memory during these drink paroxysms, and questioned business transactions and bargains he made at this time. On one occasion he went to New York and made foolish purchases which he could not recall. On several occasions he discharged valuable workmen, and when he became sober took them back, unable to account for such acts. These and other very strange acts continued to increase with every drink excess. At such times he was reticent, and seemed to be sensible and conscious, and did these strange acts in a sudden, impulsive way. The forged note was offered boldly, and no effort was made to conceal his presence or destination. When arrested he was alarmed and could not believe that he had done so foolish an act. This was a clear case of alcoholic trance, in which all the facts sustained his assertion of no conscious memory of the crime.

In these three cases the correctness of the prisoners' assertions of no memory were verified by all the facts and circumstances of the crimes. The mere statement of a person accused of crime, that he had no memory of the act, should lead to a careful examination, and be only accepted as a fact when it is supported by other evidence.

The following case illustrates the difficulty of supporting a prisoner's statement of no memory when it is used for purposes of deception :

MANSLAUGHTER.

Case E.—An inebriate killed a man in a fight, and was sentenced to prison for life. He claimed no memory or recollection of the act. I found that, when drinking, he seemed conscious of all his surroundings, and was always anxious to conceal his real condition; and if anything had happened while in this state, he was very active to repair and hush it up. He was at times quite delirious when under the influence of spirits, but would stop at once if anyone came along that he respected. He would, after acting wildly, seem to grow sober at once, and do everything to restore the disorder he had created. The crime was an accident, and at once he attempted concealment, ran away, changed his clothing, and tried to disguise his identity; when arrested, claimed no memory or consciousness of the act. This claim was clearly not true, and contradicted by the facts.

MURDER.

In a recent case, F. shot his partner in business while both were intoxicated, and displayed great cunning to conceal the crime and person; then, after elaborate preparations, went away. He made the same claim of defence, which was unsupported by any other evidence or facts in his previous life. He was executed. Of course it is possible for the trance state to come on suddenly, and crime be committed at this time; still, so far, all the cases studied show that this condition existed before, and was the product of a growth beginning in brief blanks of a few moments and extending to hours' and days' duration. Unless the facts indicated the trance state before the crime was committed, it would be difficult to establish this condition for the first time, followed and associated with the crime.

I think in most of these cases, where this defence is set up, there will be found certain groups of cases that have common physical conditions of degeneration. These groups of cases I have divided from a clinical standpoint, the value of which will be more as an outline for future studies.

Probably the largest number of criminal inebriates who claim loss of memory as a defence for their acts are the alcoholic dements. This class are the chronic inebriates of long duration, persons who have naturally physical and mental defects, and who have used spirits to excess for years. This, with bad training in early life, bad surroundings, and bad nutrition, have made them of necessity unsound, and liable to have many and complex brain defects. Such persons are always more or less without consciousness or realization of their acts. They act automatically only, governed by the lowest and most transient impulses. (Crimes of all kinds are generally accidents growing out of the surroundings, without premeditation or plan.) They are incapable of sane reasoning or appreciation of the results of their conduct. The crime is unreasoned, and general indifference marks all their acts afterwards. The claim of no memory in such cases has always a reasonable basis of truth in the physical conditions of the person. Mania is very rarely present, but delusions and morbid impulses of a melancholic type always exist. The mind, like the body, is exhausted, depressed, and acts along lines of least resistance.

The second group of criminals who claim no memory are those where the crime is unusual, extraordinary, and unforeseen. Persons who are inebriates suddenly commit murder, steal, or do some criminal act that is foreign to all previous conduct. In such cases the trance condition may have been present for some time before and escaped any special notice, except the mere statement of the person that he could not recollect his acts. The unusual nature of the crime, committed by persons who never before by act or thought gave any indication of it, is always a factor sustaining the claim of no memory. The explosive, unreasoning character of crime always points to mental unsoundness and incapacity of control.

A third group of criminals urge this statement of no memory, who, unlike the first group, are not imbeciles, generally. They are positive inebriates, drinking to excess, but not to stupor, who suddenly commit crime with the most idiotic coolness and indifference, never manifesting the slightest appreciation of the act as wrong, or likely to be followed by punishment. Crime committed by this class is never concealed, and the criminal's after-conduct and appearance gives no intimation that he is aware of what he has done. These cases have been termed moral paralytics, and the claim of the trance state may be very likely true.

A fourth group of cases where memory is claimed

to be absent occurs in dipsomaniacs and periodical inebriates, who have distinct free intervals of sobriety. This class begin to drink to great excess at once, then drink less for a day or more, and begin as violently as ever again. In this short interval of moderate drinking some crime is committed of which they claim not to have any recollection.

Other cases have been noted where a condition of mental irritation or depression preceded the drink explosion, and the crime was committed during this premonitory period and before they drank to excess. The strong probability of trance at this period is sustained by the epileptic character of such conduct afterwards. The trance state may be justly termed a species of *aura*, or brain paralysis, which precedes the explosion.

In some instances, before the drink storm comes on, the person's mind would be filled with the most intense suspicions, fears, delusions, and exhibit a degree of irritation and perturbation unusual and unaccountable. Intense excitement or depression, from no apparent cause, prevails, and during this period some crime may be committed; then comes the drink paroxysm, and later all the past is a blank. Trance is very likely to be present at this time.

The future of such cases depends on the removal of the causes which made them what they are. The possibility of permanent restoration is very promising in most cases. How far alcoholic trance exists in criminal cases is unknown, but the time has come when such a claim by criminals cannot be ignored, and must be the subject of serious inquiry. Such a claim cannot be treated as a mere subterfuge to avoid puuishment, but should receive the same attention that a claim of insanity or self-defence would. This is only an outliuc view of a very wide and most practical field of medico-legal research, largely unknown, which can be seen in every court-room of the land. These cases appeal to us for help aud recognition, and the highest dictates of humanity and justice demand of us an accurate study and comprehension of their nature and character.

The following summary of the leading facts in this trance condition will be a standpoint for other and more minute investigations:

1st. The trance state in inebriety is a distinct brain conditiou that exists beyond all question or doubt.

2nd. This brain state is one in which all memory and consciousness of acts or words are suspended, the persou going about automatically, giving little or no evidence of his real condition.

3rd. The higher brain-centres controlling consciousness are suspended, as in the somnambulistic or hypnotic state. The duration of this state may be from a few moments to several days, and the person at this time may appear conscious and act naturally, and along the line of his ordinary life.

4th. During this trance period crime against person or property may be committed without any motive or apparent plan, usually unforeseen and unexpected. When accurately studied, such a crime will lack in the details and methods of execution, and also show want of consciousness of the nature and results of such acts.

5th. When this condition passes away, the acts and conduct of the person show that he did not remember what he had done before. Hence his denial of all recollection of past events, and his changed manner, confirm or deny his statements.

6th. When such cases come under judicial inquiry the statement of the prisoner requires a scientific study before it can be accepted as a probable fact. It cannot be simulated, but is susceptible of proof beyond the comprehension of the prisoner.

7th. In such a state crime and criminal impulses are the result of unknown and unforeseen influences, and the person in this condition is dangerous and an irresponsible madman.

8th. This condition should be fully recognised by court and jury, and the measure of responsibility and punishment suited to each case. They should not be punished as criminals, nor should they be liberated as sane men. They should be housed and confined in hospitals.

CHAPTER VI.

CEREBRAL AUTOMATISM OR TRANCE.

THAT an automatic action of the brain may exist and continue for an indefinite period has been pretty well established. It may arise from somnambulism, epilepsy, catalepsy, post-hypnotic conditions, and more especially from the action of alcohol. It is not unlikely that great concentrativeness of a mental order may determine a like state, though only temporary. A merchant in Melbourne for days was oblivious of the fact that he had a wife and family, although living in the house. He attended to business daily, and in no way revealed his abnormal ideas to those about him. At the end of a week, having had his drink cut off, he suddenly became conscious and alive to the discovery that something unusual had happened. Mr. W. had been drinking brandy for nearly three weeks. A lady, married, young, delicately constituted, and possessing great beauty, indulged in drink-storms three or four times a year. During the attacks her conduct was very curious. In turn she would set fire to the house, throw weapons at her husband or friends, indulge in midnight rides, prefer serious charges against her relatives, and, generally speaking, make matters exceedingly lively. This trance, or insane development, frequently disappeared in an hour, and the patient returned to her normal condition. She was then a most refined and charming woman. There is every reason to believe that the acts of many testators are carried out under the influence of cerebral automatism. A testator is looked upon as sane if he is 'of sound mind, memory, and understanding,' and the converse if not. In testamentary cases no question touching the rightness or wrongness or the nature and quality of the act arises, supposing a man subject to trance-attacks makes a will while under the new influence. Again, assuming his aberration to be known by an interested party, how simple a matter it would be to suggest the execution of another will in favour of the conspirator! What a difficult case it would be for a jury to decide! and how could they know what state the man was in on a certain date? Yet the decision rests with them. In criminal and testamentary cases a conjecture as to what was in the mind of the prisoner or testator has to be jumped at. The law, however, in an inquisition, demands that the conduct shall be judged; and further, 'is the patient incapable of managing himself and his affairs?' In criminal cases the legal test is that a criminal is considered sane when he committed the crime if 'he then knew the nature and quality of the act, and that it was wrong.' To all appearance a man in a trance-like state may indicate in no way to the ordinary observer any abnormality in his conduct, yet the man is as irresponsible as the most violent maniac for any act he may perform. How are such cases to be distinguished, and what bearing would evidence of such symptoms have upon a case as the law now stands?

Not for an instant would such a defence be listened to as the English law at present understands insanity. Dr. Crothers gives some interesting histories of cases of cerebral automatism that were under his care, as follow:

Case I.—E.: Born in Ireland. Parents moderate drinkers; was engaged as a fireman on a North river steamer for several years after coming to this country. At the age of twenty-one he drank to intoxication. Had drank moderately from sixteen years of age. When twenty-four he became a bar-keeper, and soon after began a career as gambler, boxer, and friend of the prize-ring. He acted as a trainer for prize-fighters, drinking to intoxication at intervals, in the meantime using beer very freely. He prided himself on his strength, and used every means for physical development. When thirty years of age he went to San Francisco, and for the next five years was alternately a miner, speculator, gambler, and prize-fighter. Returning east, he kept a low hotel in Buffalo, then failed, and became a drummer for a liquor house. He drank all this time regularly, was more frequently intoxicated, had attacks of delirium tremens, and was either very happy or very irritable when under the influence of drink. When thirty-eight years of age, he began to be stupid at times, and trembled excessively for a few hours before he could regain possession of himself after a paroxysm of drink; slept badly, and was anæmic.

One year after, his brother (who is a temperate man, and apparently very candid and truthful) noticed that he seemed not to know what was going on when he had drank for some time, although he appeared and talked in a rational way. He had no recollection of what had happened afterwards. From his own statement, which was confirmed by the observation of others, he would lose all consciousness of the present, and after a day or two awake quite as suddenly, and all the interval be a blank to him. In this interval he would transact business, and act as usual, his friends not noticing anything peculiar. On one occasion he acted as umpire at a sparring match, deciding correctly and giving satisfaction without any memory of it whatever. The last he remembered was a proposition that he should be umpire, which was followed by a glass of brandy, and a sudden oblivion of all other events of time and occasion. Going to Rochester one day, he drank hard, and lost all memory of events for three days following, when he awoke in a hotel in New York. His friends said he had a 'fit,' or short paroxysm of stupor and trembling, from which he recovered, and went about as usual, only a little more reticent; his eyes had a wild expression, and he frequently stopped and gazed as if wrapped up in some abstraction. He made sales and collections correctly for his employers during this time, but ate and drank very little. On another occasion (which was amply confirmed by other evidence) he went to New York to arrange for a sparring match, and after drinking, lost all recollection of any further events. Had a paroxysm of trembling and stupor, awoke, went on with the business, acted as judge, and managed the exhibition well, and seemed in full possession of his faculties. Arranged for another match, and advised sensibly and clearly about it. He would not talk about other matters, and seemed lost when strange topics were mentioned. He affirmed that he was going to stop drinking, went to bed, and after a heavy sleep woke with no recollection of this time, which occupied over three days. Several other similar events took place, only not of so long duration. During the last year a marked failure of all his faculties was apparent. When he was admitted at Binghampton, he had a vague look; his eyes were largely dilated, associated with a marked abstractedness of manner. He seemed in a daze, and moved about mechanically. Twenty hours after he awoke and inquired how and when he came, and said he remembered nothing from the time of going to bed, after having drank very hard, nearly three days before. He remained in the asylum for six weeks, then returned to Buffalo, and died three months later of some obscure affection of the brain. The sudden cutting off of memory and consciousness, and the automatic character of the actions after, not apparent to those about him, were the striking points of this case.

Case II.—T. H.: Father healthy up to thirty years of age, when he became a drunkard and died soon after. Grandfather also died about the same time from inebriety contracted late in life. T. H. was a successful business man, and during the war he occupied a very responsible position, necessitating many irregularities of living, from which he began to drink for temporary relief; at the age of forty-nine he began to use brandy regularly for its effects; later he was intoxicated, and showed a marked susceptibility to its effects. It was observed that after a few days' drinking he could resist and break away from its use for an interval of a few weeks; then the paroxysms would return and he would again be powerless to control himself. The free intervals grew shorter and the paroxysms more severe. Giving up business, he attempted to stop drinking, without avail. In 1868 he was sent to Binghampton for six months, and returned home quite well, remaining so for three years. The death of his wife and grief caused him to drink again to excess, followed by an attack of delirium tremens, after which his friends noticed a change of disposition and a loss of memory, lasting for uncertain intervals. He would remain sober for a long time, and be very positive that he would always be so. Then he would become morose, irritable, and restless, and drink soon after, and could never realize that these emotions always preceded a paroxysm of drink. Two or more glasses of whisky would make him oblivious to all memory of passing events. He would go at once to his son's store and aid him energetically, and show excellent judgment in advising him, giving but little evidence of his being under the influence of alcohol. He would insist on the most rigid rules of business and living, and act them out in his own life. His eyes were flashing and his manner was hurried and flushed, although sensible and clear. When he drank in the presence of strangers he insisted on great precision of etiquette, always frowning on any low, rough language. He drank usually strong brandies. When overcome by the effects, he showed great deliberation and forethought about his condition and where he should sleep, but when he awoke all memory of the past was gone. On one occasion, when drinking in New York, he remembered nothing beyond a certain point. In this time he witnessed an assault which ended in a murder—went before the coroner, testified clearly as to the facts, and gave no impression of his actual condition; but two days after he awoke with no recollection of this event, and could give no evidence to confirm his previous testimony. The lawyers thought it deception or an attempt to shield the prisoner, although he could have no possible motive. These periods of unconsciousness increased and followed every protracted debauch. His mind failed, and when the paroxysm was on him he drank brandy every two hours with the regularity of medicine. The periods of unconsciousness varied sometimes from two hours to three days, and were more frequent. He grows more and more irritable and full of changing emotions. His mind is more stupid, and his memory is faulty on all events of everyday life. To the casual observer he seems in full possession of all his senses, and even when drinking seems fully conscious of every event about him.

Case III.—O.: Born of temperate parents, was indulged in luxurious food in early life and worked hard on the farm. At fifteen had an attack of dyspepsia while at college; this trouble continued, and he suffered at intervals acutely. He began to study music, and at twenty became an organist, and worked very hard for the next four or five years, living more and more irregularly in all his habits. He used medicine of all kinds, had an attack of malaria, and finally found relief in patent bitters and compounds of whisky, which he took very freely. From this time on he used spirits constantly, sometimes to intoxication, and always was more or less under their influence. At thirty years of age he was a drunkard, being intoxicated nearly every night, yet he followed his profession with assiduity. Many desperate exertions were made to relieve himself of this impulse to drink, which always ended in failure. He had an attack of alcoholic convulsions after a long debauch, and remained sober for over six months after; when he began to drink again he suddenly lost all memory of events, and many hours later awoke, finding he had gone about as usual without attracting any special attention from his friends. These periods of oblivion returned more frequently, and seemed to follow every excess of drink. He drank less, but with no change. On one occasion he was to play at a concert; on the way to the hall he drank, and lost all memory of present events. To his friends he appeared dazed, although answering all questions, and playing with skill and a kind of wildness that was apparent only to his intimate friends. On another occasion, while playing an interlude at a funeral, he whispered to a friend to get him some whisky or he would have to play 'Yankee Doodle'—the impulse was so strong that he showed agony in restraining himself. The whisky was procured and he went on more steadily, but at the close of the piece he dashed off in a most fantastic musical impromptu, after which he went home staggering and talking in a childish tone; was put to bed, and awoke next morning with no memory whatever of what had passed. At another time he lost all memory while on his way to church one Sunday morning after he had drank quite freely, and on Tuesday afternoon, two days later, awoke in a city over a hundred miles away, and found he had been negotiating for the purchase of instruments with an organ manufactory. He had no memory or the least impression of anything which had taken place in the meantime. To his friends he appeared dull and abstracted, sometimes failing to recognise them, and rarely ever speaking to anyone unless on business. At a concert one night he created an immense sensation by his rapidly changing music, from grave to the most airy, light fantastic sounds. In habits he was variable, and his mind was visionary and changeable—full of whims, etc. At present this case has made little or no improvement, each paroxysm of drink being attended with this strange condition of automatic action.

Case IV.—A.: Merchant in active business, whose parents had both been temperate and healthy. He grew up on the sugar plantation of his uncle, and drank wine freely at the table after dinner. When eighteen years old the war broke out, and he entered the Southern army as a soldier. A few months later he was injured by a shell, and remained unconscious for many hours. After this he suffered severely from malaria, and was given large doses of quinine, which resulted in permanent deafness. He was discharged and went to the plantation, and began to drink brandy after eating, regularly. After the war closed he went to New Orleans, and began business in a commission house. After an attack of yellow fever he drank steadily, with great relief from all the neuralgia and other entailments following the fever. He was easily depressed from slight causes, had a variable appetite, smoked incessantly, and lived with great irregularity. At times he was able to restrain his desire for alcohol, then all at once an impulse to drink would come over him that was irresistible. At twenty-eight he noticed that memory of plans and events would suddenly leave him when he drank a certain amount, and only return after a longer or shorter interval. This increased, and after a time he found that he went about transacting business which he could not remember after. As an illustration: After a severe attack of drinking, he was at his desk making out a bill, when a sudden blank came over him. Two days later he awoke in his room, and found that he had gone on with business as usual, making many sales and manifesting good judgment. To his friends he was under the influence of drink, but not in any way peculiar. At another time he displayed a great deal of energy and tact in completing the sale of some cotton, and bought large quantities of rice with a reckless spirit that alarmed his friends, but which proved a good venture after. He had no consciousness of this event, or the slightest recollection of what he had done. His mind seemed to fail, and at times he was in a half-conscious condition, and seemed not to realize where he was. He was a careful man and kept a daily record of events, but these periods were blanks which he could never recall. He remained in the asylum for six months, and recovered, and is now a planter in Georgia, in good health, not having relapsed for three years. In this case nothing peculiar or different from the others appeared, except a degree of mental strength that seemed out of proportion to his actual state when suffering in this way.

Case V.—O. A. was a captain in the army and a lawyer by profession. His early history was not ascertained. While leading his battery in an engagement he was wounded in the head by a fragment of a shell. He also suffered from a severe concussion from which he was made unconscious, which was followed by acute delirium for nearly a month. Recovering, he became a paroxysmal drunkard. Five years later he reformed and continued sober for two years. Then from grief and trouble he drank again, and for a time was unconscious and lost memory of all events. A few months later drank again, and the same oblivion of memory of time and events followed, with no appearance of his condition to his friends. From this time on his wife made a careful study of these events, noting them with great accuracy. One of the most remarkable was as follows: While preparing a case for trial (in which he was deeply engaged, and had lain awake for several nights in nervous anticipation), he drank a few glasses of whisky before going into the court-room, and became oblivious. Over thirty hours after he awoke with no recollection of what had happened. During this time he had conducted the trial with clearness, charged the jury, and made a good argument before the judge, then went home and wrote out a long argument for an appeal, went to sleep, and all this time was a blank. He not unfrequently went about for two days, to his friends perfectly conscious, although under the influence of liquor, and yet perfectly oblivious to everything. These blanks came and went without any premonition, and suddenly. Sometimes he would appear dull and stupid, at other times very lively and extremely energetic. He would either seem to have a great purpose before him, or be without any object, but never appear devoid of the fullest consciousness of all passing events and circumstances. These occasions would come from different quantities of alcohol; sometimes a single glass, then a season of hard drinking would bring them on. He is very much broken in health; is nervous and anæmic; has distinct cravings for alcohol, which he cannot resist unless under peculiar circumstances. For over a year he has been sober, but walks and talks much during sleep.

Case VI.—A. H. is an editor, whose mother was an epileptic, and who began to drink from irregularities in the army. He drinks at distinct intervals, particularly if he is depressed, then recovers, and goes about clear and temperate. Periods of blanks in memory come on quite frequently now, in which he will go about able to do some business, although imperfectly, and have no recollection after. He can only write short paragraphs while in this condition; long articles are broken and full of changes. He will become oblivious suddenly at some unexpected moment, and from this time go on for hours, uutil he can have a sleep, before he recovers. I noted this condition very carefully some months ago. He had drank for four days steadily, then all at once put on this abstracted air, and had a vague, pointless way of talking and acting. He would not hold any connected conversation on any topic but his everyday business; here his thoughts were clear and rational. He listened and took notes in a vague, uncertain way, and wrote in a mechanical form and style. After, he could not recall the slightest hint of these events. This was like the others in all points, although the condition of unconsciousness was manifest in vagueness and uncertainty that could not be mistaken.

Another case has lately come under my care, whose

history was made out by a physician, and is undoubtedly correct. He inherited a defective brain and nerve power, and drank constantly. At twenty he was a confirmed opium-eater, at thirty reformed, and at thirty-five began again to use stimulants very freely. His friends noticed that he was absent-minded at times, and not like himself. These periods were found to be blanks of memory, which he could not recall. On many occasions he went away, made business arrangements, and had no recollection of it after. It was noticed that he only performed or carried out what had been previously determined. As, for instance, his partner with him arranged to purchase a certain class of goods in the future. Two days after, while drinking and oblivious in memory, he went away and made the purchase, returned, and did not realize or know about it until informed by some friends. This man will play on the piano for hours, and appear sensible of the surroundings, and yet have no memory of it. An intimate friend of a noted senator, now dead, mentioned a similar instance which occurred during the later years of the senator's life, where, in making a tour of his district extending over three or four weeks, in which he spoke from four to six times a week, drinking nearly all the time, the last two weeks would be all oblivion to him, no recollection remaining, although he seemed as usual, made the same speeches, and appeared in no way different, except a little heavy and abstracted. An eminent Baptist clergyman informed me that he had noted many instances of persons who, while the rite of baptism was being performed, were oblivious to all that was said and done. This he ascribed to nervous fear, but it was noted by an automatic condition of mind and body very similar to some of the cases mentioned above. In a recent article by Dr. C. A. Hughes, of St. Louis, on 'Cerebral Automatism arising from an Epileptic Origin,' mention is made of cases having similar conditions, with observations that bear directly on this subject, from which I quote: 'I was once consulted by an individual who, while standing at the desk engaged in writing a note, was taken with an epileptic attack, but nevertheless he affixed his signature and the date to the note accurately, without any memory after a certain part of the letter. He considered in his mind what he should say, then all was a blank; twenty minutes after he read what he had written, which was correct. Here the mind had gone on automatically. Many paralytic cases have distinct periods of unconsciousness, which are only to be discovered by a careful observation and inquiry.

'I had another case still more significant. A young lady who had epileptic fits at the menstrual period would, after the paroxysm, remain unconscious for two or more days, and during this time would do the most elaborate embroidery, and paint different things, yet have no recollection after. The only thing peculiar was her determined aversion to see any company, otherwise she seemed in full possession of all her faculties.'

Dr. Hammond has mentioned a case of a man who for eight days continued in an epileptic trance, and went about automatically, doing business, and calling on his friends with absolutely no recollection of it after. From his appearance and conversation, nothing strange was noted. Dr. Carpenter relates the following incident, to show that the mind in health may be so absorbed as to lose all memory of the present, or consciousness of the surroundings. 'John Stuart Mill would very often be so absorbed in some topic as to be utterly oblivious of anything which happened in his walk from his office to his home, a distance of two miles. On one occasion an accident occurred, and he was delayed by the crowd for nearly an hour, yet he never realized anything about it, or had any recollection of what had taken place. The walking and surroundings of the man were not recognised by the higher cerebral centres. As in somnambulism, the higher cerebral and other centres act automatically, and the memory fails to register the events.'

An instance is recorded of a somnambulist whose night-dress caught fire while he was walking about. With apparent judgment and coolness he threw himself on a bed and extinguished the flames, resumed his walk, and next morning had no memory of the event, and wondered greatly how his dress had become so charred. This was a clear case of cerebral automatism or trance, where the knowledge of right and wrong seemed present, although consciousness was obliterated. Here the higher cerebral centres seem to follow the lead of the lower. The most common illustration of this condition is afforded by the blanks of memory in epileptics. Here the patient will stop short, stare fixedly for a few moments, then recover and go on with no memory of this blank. In the later stages this sudden blank will be followed by confusion and apathy for hours or days, and when the consciousness returns little or no memory of these periods will remain, and during this time the patient may do business and act rationally, so as to excite no suspicion of his real condition.

Dr. Thorne, of London, relates a case of an old army officer in the quartermaster's department who for days after a *grand mal* would go on with his work with great exactness, and give no indications of his condition other than heaviness and a vacant look, but if opposed he would be wildly dangerous and insane; after an interval of some ten days he would recover his senses, and have no recollection of anything that had passed.

Dr. J. Hughlings Jackson, in a long paper 'On Temporary Mental Disorders after Epileptic Paroxysms,' in the West Riding Reports for 1875, says: 'I think it probable that there is a transitory epileptic paroxysm in every case of mental automatism occurring in epileptics before their mental automatism sets in. During this paroxysm there may be an internal discharge, too slight to cause obvious external effects, but strong enough to put out of use for a time more or less of the highest nerve centres. In other words, loss of control of the lower centres permits the automatic action. Often, after slight epileptic seizures, automatic actions may be developed, as, for example, playing a well-practised tune; the playing may go on while the person is more or less unconscious.'

Dr. Jackson mentions a case of a gentleman who frequently lost all memory of events for hours, and did not seem peculiar to his friends, except by wanting to pay twice for anything he had bought, having forgot the first payment, and showing a degree of forgetfulness that was strange. The form of automatism depends on the disposition of the man. He might have a train of murderous thoughts which he would proceed to execute. Or he might have conceived the most absurd irrational theories, which would have involved him in crime, and for which he would have been punished, and of which he was thoroughly unconscious at the time. Here all the materials for crime are abundant, and the patient would be held responsible, although in no way conscious of his actions. Paralysis of the cerebral functions, or, as Dr. Hughlings Jackson puts it, ' conditions of hyperæmia, vasomotor paralysis from reflex action, or from lesions of the controlling centres, may be present.' Lunatics who have recovered after a long attack of insanity very often have little or no recollection of the events which have transpired during this time, although they appeared to have lucid intervals, and acted and talked quite rationally.

There are certain conditions of the brain in which the action of the higher centres may be more or less automatic, and go on without even the intervention of consciousness. A constant repetition of certain mental actions results in their becoming registered organically in the brain centres, and after a time these thoughts, which were first performed consciously by the individual, ultimately become reflex and respond to the recognised stimulus without consciousness, independently of any effort or intervention of former stimulus. Dr. Beard of New York discusses this subject so very clearly in a paper entitled ' Scientific Basis of Delusions,' read before the New York Medico-Legal Society, that I take pleasure in quoting several passages which clearly explain many of these phenomena and similar conditions under the name of cerebral trance.

'The theory of the nature of this trance is that it is a functional disease of the nervous system, in which the cerebral activity is concentrated in some limited region of the brain, with suspension of the activity of the rest of the brain, and consequent loss of volition. Like other functional nervous diseases, it may be induced either physically or psychically, that is, by influences that act on the nervous system, or on the mind; more frequently the latter, sometimes both combined. . . .

'Among the physical causes are injuries to the brain, the exhaustion of protracted disease, or of starvation, or of over-exertion, anæsthetics, alcohol, and many drugs, and certain cerebral diseases. . . . In sleep-walking the cerebral activity, which during ordinary sleep is more or less lowered throughout the brain, is suddenly concentrated in some limited region; the subject is then under dominion of this restricted region of the brain; the activity of the rest of the brain being suspended, he runs and walks about like an automaton. The popular term "absent-minded," as applied to those who become so absorbed in thought as to be unconscious as to what is going on about them, expresses with partial correctness the real state of the brain during an attack of this kind. In nearly all conditions of trance the subject, on coming out of a trance, has no recollection of his experience in it; but in some cases, on again entering into the trance, he resumes the experience of his previous attack where he left off, as though no active life had intervened.'

In three murder trials occurring in Connecticut

during a few years past, the defence indicated continued drunkenness and general abstractedness of manner for a long time before the tragedies, and the prisoners stoutly disclaimed all knowledge of memory of the events. These were undoubtedly cases of suspended memory and cerebral trance, and as such the measure of responsibility would have been greatly lessened.

Dr. Carpenter, in his discussion of automatic cerebration, remarks as follows: 'I have noticed some cases of drunkenness which were clearly traced to inherited neurosis, where a suspension of memory or consciousness was noted, which came on unexpectedly, and then the patient was a victim to morbid impulses which he never realized, or had any recollection of after.'

In a recapitulation, the following may be mentioned:

1st. Loss of memory and consciousness may come on in inebriety, and the patient give little or no evidence of his actual condition.

2nd. This symptom is common to epilepsy and other conditions of the brain, arising from various causes not well understood.

3rd. It is practically of the greatest moment to distinguish the presence of this state in instances of contested cases where crime or important events have followed.

4th. All cases of crime, with a history of inebriety, should be carefully studied for evidence of this condition, which, if present, will open a new field of medico-legal study of great practical importance.

CHAPTER VII.

ALCOHOLISM AND ITS LEGAL RELATIONS.

BRITISH jurists have not so far consented to the inclusion of alcoholism as a plea in law. And it is not difficult to understand the position adopted towards this disease, seeing that only very recently has this form of malady been recognised by the profession of medicine. That the time is fast approaching when a *modus vivendi* will have to be established by the legal and medical professions in dealing with permanent alcoholic disorders and their sequences in the shape of criminal offences is certain. There are circumstances which, even in the present undeveloped state of the law upon this point, admit of release from obligations entered upon in a state of drunkenness. A contract is in law avoidable by proof of want of consideration, constraint, error, personal incapacity, fraud, etc. As J. R. McIlraith puts it: 'Of these, the only heads we are concerned with here are incapacity and error, constraint and fraud. It may, then, be laid down that if the person seeking to be relieved from his obligation can establish that by reason of his drunkenness he was (1) incapable for legal acts at the time of contracting, or (2) induced to oblige himself under circumstances establishing essential error, constraint, or fraud, then he would be held justified in refusing to fulfil his obligation.'

In 1593, Sir Edward Coke defined a drunkard as 'Voluntarius dæmon,' *i.e.*, a man possessed or dominated by an evil spirit not his own, and who is present at his own invitation. Insanity being really the condition existent, and admittedly so, no privilege attaches to the same in favour of the alcoholist, for, he adds, the drunkard 'hath no privilege thereby, but what hurt or ill soever he doeth his drunkennesse doth aggravate it.' This is coincided in by Lord Bacon, who wrote : ' If a madman commit a felony, he shall not lose his life for it, because his infirmity came by the act of God ; but if a drunken man commit a felony, he shall not be excused, because his imperfection came by his own default.' This is pretty well the state of things now existing. It will be seen that differentiation of no kind whatever is provided for the man who is diseased through either the hereditary or the acquired forms of alcoholism, and therefore he is liable to all punishments equally with the man who purposely indulges in fits of intoxication.

1.—ENGLISH LAW IN CIVIL CASES.

A. How far does Drunkenness imply Legal Incapacity ?

That drunkenness is an element whence a man's incapacity to do legal acts may be inferred, is undoubtedly part of the English Common Law. Thus, Lord Coke expressly includes 'drunkard' as one instance of the class of persons called *non compos mentis*, and persons suffering from delirium tremens, which is frequently the result of habits of intoxication, have always been held to come within another of Lord Coke's instances, namely, *lunaticus qui gaudet lucidis intervallis* (see Beverley's case, 4 Co. R. 124, b.). So Pothier, in his 'Treatise on Obligations' (pt. i. c. i. § i. art. 4), says: 'It is clear that drunkenness when it exists to such a degree as to occasion a temporary loss of the reasoning powers, renders a person incapable of contracting while thus affected, since such affection renders him incapable of consenting.' *Cp.* the old (1672) Scotch case of Lord Haltoun *v.* Earl of Northesk (Morr. 13,384). Every person, however, is presumed in law to be of sound mind and capable for legal acts unless the contrary appear, and therefore that a man is *non compos mentis*, and unable to be his own guardian, must in each case be strictly proved. For this purpose it is not sufficient merely to establish the fact of drunkenness. What must be shown is such a degree of drunkenness as would deprive the person of his power of reasoning and prevent his being a free and voluntary agent. If, however, a person is clearly proved to be *non compos mentis* and unable to exercise proper deliberation in regard to his affairs, the law makes a presumption in his favour, and endeavours to prevent his sustaining loss or damage through his incapacity. As Lord Tenterden, C.J., once said: 'It is very important that courts of justice should afford protection to those individuals who are unfortunately unable to be their own guardians' (Sentance *v.* Poole, 3 Car. & P. 3).

B. *How far are a Drunkard's Contracts avoidable?*

Secondly, that the fact of drunkenness may be important when a person seeks to be freed from an obligation on the ground of error, constraint, or fraud, is established by many cases. Thus, in Butler *v.* Mulvihall (1 Bligh, H. L. 137) it was held that a lease obtained by fraud and imposition from a person in a state of intoxication was void, and in Shaw *v.* Thackray (1 Sm. & Gif. 540) the V.C. said : ' Where there has been improper contrivance to procure a deed and a suit afterwards instituted upon it, the Court has dismissed the bill.' So in the American case of Prentice *v.* Achorn (2 Paige 30), where a trust conveyance of a farm was sought to be retracted, the jury found that the deed was fraudulently and improperly obtained from the grantor at a time when he was, by reason of intoxication, wholly incompetent to exercise proper deliberation, and it was accordingly set aside as being fraudulent and void. In such cases it is not even necessary always to prove actual fraud, for under certain circumstances fraud will be implied. Thus, in Rich *v.* Sydenham (1 Ca. in Ch. 202) a bond had been given by defendant when drunk for £1,600 in security of an actual loan of £90, and the plaintiff got no relief, ' not so much as for the principal he had really lent,' the difference in amounts making it sufficiently clear that he had been guilty of fraud in taking the bond. *Cp.* Wiltshire *v.* Marshall (14 L. T. 396), Gregory *v.* Fraser (3 Camp. 453), Brandon *v.* Old (3 C. & P. 440), and Nagle *v.* Baylor (3 Dr. & War. Ch. R. 60). In Scotland there are cases to the same effect; see especially Couston *v.* Miller (24 D. 607), Gairdner *v.* Tennant (3 Bro. Sup. 162), Jardine *v.* Elliott (Hume 684) and Hunter *v.* Stevenson (Hume 686).

C. *Fraud implied from Drunkenness.*

It is very important to note that something more than mere intoxication must be proved in order to establish error, constraint, or fraud. Thus, in Cory *v.*

Cory (1 Ves. Sen. 19), the question was whether it was sufficient to set aside an agreement that one of the parties was drunk at the time, and the Lord Chancellor thought it was not, unless some unfair advantage was taken. So in Johnson *v.* Medlicott (3 P. Wms. 130 n.), Sir Joseph Jekyll is reported to have said that the having been in drink is not any reason to relieve a man against any deed or agreement gained from him when in those circumstances, for this were to encourage drunkenness: *secus* if through the management or contrivance of him who gained the deed, the party from whom such deed has been gained was drawn into drink. Again, in Cooke *v.* Clayworth (18 Ves. 15), Sir W. Grant says: 'I think a Court of Equity ought not to give its assistance to a person who has obtained an agreement or deed from another in a state of intoxication; and, on the other hand, ought not to assist a person to get rid of any agreement or deed merely upon the ground of his having been intoxicated at the time,' and these words are approved by the V.C. in Shaw *v.* Thackray (1 Sm. & Gif. 540), who adds: 'The course of the Courts in these cases is generally not to interfere. But where there has been improper contrivance to procure a deed and a suit afterwards instituted upon it, the Court has dismissed the bill.' With regard to what Sir John Stuart there says about the Courts not interfering on either side in such cases, reference may be made to Cragg *v.* Holme (18 Ves. 14, n.), where the M.R. seems to have dismissed a bill for specific performance of an agreement made in a state of intoxication, though no advantage was taken, on the ground that the Court would not act on either side in cases of intoxication.

This custom, however, seems to have fallen into disuse, so that Cragg v. Holme is of no importance now. Before leaving this subject it may be well to mention that there is a Scotch case (Anon. Feb. 9th, 1682, 2 Bro. Sup. 19) where it was pleaded that the grantor of a bond was extremely drunk and incapable to consider or consent when he subscribed it, and it was held that this plea was insufficient, because it did not allege that the receiver of the bond did deceitfully procure the grantor to be drunk.

D. *The Real Question is one of Capacity or Incapacity.*

On looking into the cases in which the element of drunkenness has been the main issue, one cannot help observing that they nearly all turn upon the question of fraud and not on the want of legal capacity. This hesitation to plead incapacity was not unwarranted. The rule which formerly prevailed was that no man of full age might in any plea in law stultify himself and disable his own person for that 'when he recovers his memory he cannot know what he did when he was *non compos mentis*' (Lord Coke in Beverley's case, 4 Co. R. 123 b.; *cp*. Kent's Comms., p. 45). This rule, however, in its full strictness is no longer law. Thus, in Molton v. Camroux (2 Ex. R. 501), Pollock, C.B., says: 'But the rule, as laid down by Littleton and Coke, has, no doubt, in modern times been relaxed, and unsoundness of mind (as also intoxication) would now be a good defence to an action upon a contract, if it could be shown that the defendant was not of capacity to contract, and the plaintiff knew it,' and in the same case, on appeal, Patteson, J., said (4 Ex. R. 19): 'The old doctrine was, that a man could not set up his own lunacy, though such as that he did not know what he was about in contracting, and the same doctrine was applied to drunkenness. . . . Modern cases have qualified it, and enabled a man, or his representatives, to show that he was so lunatic, or drunk, as not to know what he was about when he made a promise or sealed an instrument. . . . But the modern cases show that when that state of mind was unknown to the other contracting party, and no advantage was taken of the lunatic, the defence cannot prevail, especially where the contract is not merely executory, but executed in the whole or in part, and the parties cannot be restored altogether to their original position' (cp. Browne v. Joddrell, 1 Moo. & Mal. 105, per Lord Tenterden, C.J., and Dane v. Viscountess Kirkwall, 8 C. & P. 679). And in Levy v. Baker (1 Moo. & Mal. 106 n.), Best, C.J., left it to the jury to say whether the plaintiff at the time he dealt with the defendant knew of his insanity; if he did, it was a gross fraud, and the jury ought to find for the defendant. In America the old rule has also been discredited. For example, in French v. French (8 Ohio, 214), Grimke, J., says: 'It was once supposed to be the law that a deed obtained from a drunken man could not for that cause be avoided. But a more rational rule now prevails, and the law now regarding the fact of intoxication and not the cause or authority of it, and regarding that fact as a proof of a want of capacity to contract, which is one of the elements of every agreement, will interfere to relieve.' (See also Barrett v. Buxton, 2 Aikens 168, per Prentiss, J., and State Bank v. McCoy, 69 Pennsyl. St. 207, per Williams, J., and cp. 2 Kent's Comms. 452.)

E. *What constitutes Incapacity?*

It will be convenient now to consider what degree of intoxication must be proved in order to establish want of legal capacity on the part of the obligor, or implied fraud on the part of the obligee. That for this purpose it is sufficient to make out drunkenness so total as to deprive the intoxicated person of knowledge of what he is doing is undoubted. (See Molton *v.* Camroux, 2 Ex. R. 501, Gore *v.* Gibson, 13 M. & W. 625, per Pollock, C.B., and Parke, B., and ca. id. cit.) Pollock, C.B., in Gore *v.* Gibson, says: 'The result of the modern authorities is that no contract made by a person in that state (of intoxication) when he does not know the consequences of his act is binding upon him,' and Parke, B., ' Where the party, when he enters into the contract, is in such a state of drunkenness as not to know what he is doing, and particularly when it appears that this was known to the other party, the contract is void altogether, and he cannot be compelled to perform it. A person who takes an obligation from another under such circumstances is guilty of actual fraud.' So in Cooke *v.* Clayworth (18 Ves. 15) the M.R. says: ' As to that extreme state of intoxication that deprives a man of his reason, I apprehend that even at law it would invalidate a deed obtained from him while in that condition.' Again, in Hawkins *v.* Bone (4 F. & F. 313), Pollock, C.B., is reported to have said: ' The law of England is that a man is not liable on a contract alleged to have been made by him in a state in which he really was not capable of contracting. A contract involves the mutual agreement of two minds, and if a man has no mind to agree he cannot make a valid contract. If defendant did not know what he was about he is not liable,' and in Lightfoot v. Heron (3 Yo. & Col. 586), where an action had been raised to enforce a writing confirming a bargain entered into in a public-house, Alderson, B., said: 'It was proved that several glasses of liquor passed. But the question does not turn much upon that. The question is whether Heron executed the agreement under such circumstances as fairly to induce the belief that he did so without the full understanding or knowledge of what he was doing. If the defendant could show that he had not that full understanding or knowledge, the plaintiff of course would have no right to relief.' There is also a case of Fenton v. Holloway (1 Starkie, N. P. R. 126), where, on a witness stating that the agreement was entered into by F. while intoxicated, Lord Ellenborough at once ruled that the instrument was to be considered as a nullity. (See also, Hawkins v. Bone, 4 F. & F. 311 note, Story on Contracts, § 86, and Pollock on Contracts, p. 49.)

F. Cases of Difficulty.

If the drunkenness is only partial there will of course be greater difficulty in proving that the man did not know what he was doing. To prove such a state of mind would then be impossible unless there were other facts to support the contention. In Shaw v. Thackray (1 Sm. & Gif. 539) the V.C. says: 'If a man, by habits of drunkenness, has destroyed his capacity, so as to become incapable of exercising his reason or his judgment, any contract into which he may enter is invalid. If, however, he has only impaired, but not destroyed his capacity, he will not be permitted by this Court to avail himself of his own misconduct to avoid his own act.' So Parke, B., in Gore *v.* Gibson (13 M. & W. 624) says: 'If the party was only partially drunk, so that he nevertheless knew what he was about, equity would not relieve;' and Lord Tenterden in Sentance *v.* Poole (3 Car. & P. 3), says: 'The question in this case is whether the defendant P. at the time he put his name to this note which is drawn in an unusual form, it being to your order and not addressed to anyone, was or was not conscious of what he was doing, for if he was there must be a verdict for the plaintiff, but should you be satisfied that he was not conscious of what he was doing, and that he was imposed upon by reason of his imbecility of mind, you ought to find for the defendant (*cp.* Hawkins *v.* Bone, 4 F. & F. 311). Again, in Molton *v.* Cummings (4 Ex. R. 17)—a case of lunacy —the ground of the decision was that the statement in the special verdict that the party was of unsound mind did not show that he was necessarily incapable of knowing the nature of his acts, because what had to be made out was not that it was not *known*, but that it was not shown to have *existed*. *Cp.* Beavan *v.* McDonell, 23 L. J., Ex. 326 (also a case of lunacy). Reference may also be made to the cases of Cole *v.* Robins (*cit.* Bullen Nisi Prius, 168), where defendant was held entitled to give in evidence that he was made to sign when he was so drunk that he did not know what he did, and of Osmond *v.* Fitzroy (3 P. Wms. 129), where it was said: ' If a weak man gives a bond, if there be no fraud or breach of trust in the obtaining it, equity will not set it aside only for the weakness of the obligor if he be *compos mentis*, neither will the Court measure the size of a person's capacities.'

G. Complete Drunkenness absolves.

The principle underlying all the cases, whether the issue is as to the capacity to consent, or as to the voluntary nature of the consent, is the same, namely, that the party was at the time of entering into the legal act incapable of giving that free and voluntary assent thereto which the law requires. (See Gore *v.* Gibson, 13 M. & W. 625, per Pollock, C.B., and 626, per Alderson, B., Molton *v.* Camroux, 2 Ex. R. 487, Sentance *v.* Poole, 3 Car. & P. 1., and Lightfoot *v.* Heron, 3 Yo. & Col. 586.) As Pothier says (on Obligations, No. 49): 'The essence of a contract consisting in consent, it follows that a person must be capable of giving his consent, and consequently must have the use of his reason in order to be able to contract.' If, then, the drunkenness is so complete as to refute any idea of voluntary consent, it will absolve the party from the consequences of his act. As Alderson, B., puts it in Gore *v.* Gibson (*supra*) : ' It is just the same as if the defendant had written his name upon the bill in his sleep in a state of somnambulism.' And in Pitt *v.* Smith (3 Camp. 33) objection was taken to a question whether the defendant was not actually in a state of complete intoxication when he executed the agreement, and Lord Ellenborough ruled that the question could be allowed to prove that there was no contract. 'There was,' he said, ' no agreement between the parties if the defendant was intoxicated in the manner supposed when he signed this paper. He had not an agreeing mind.' To the same effect are the words of Prentiss, J., in the American case of Barrett *v.* Buxton (2 Aikens 167). The same reason, too, is at the foundation of the rule that fraud and imposition invalidate agreements, the idea being that the obligor could not under such circumstances have acted with his eyes open.

H. *Exceptional Cases.*

There would appear to be one or two exceptional cases in which drunkenness would not, even when total and known to the other party, be, except under special circumstances, allowed in bar of an action. Thus, Pollock, C.B., in Molton *v.* Camroux (2 Ex. R. 487) says: 'The law did not allow the party himself to set aside by any plea of insanity acts of a public and notorious character, such as acts done in a Court of Record and feoffments with livery of seisin, the doing or executing of which would not presumably be allowed unless the party appeared to be of sound mind.' And in the same case on appeal (4 Ex. R. 19) Patteson, J., says: 'When the state of the mind was unknown to the other contracting party, and no advantage was taken of the lunatic, the defence cannot prevail, especially where the contract is not merely executory, but executed in whole or in part, and the parties cannot be restored altogether to their original position.' So in the American case of French *v.* French (8 Ohio, 214), Grimke, J., says: 'It must be an exceedingly strong case which would authorize the annulling of an executed agreement.' Another exceptional case is as to bills of exchange. Thus, in Caulkins *v.* Fry (35 Connecticut, 170) it is said that 'as against the payer, the maker may avail himself of any defence which shows that the paper was either void or voidable, while as against a bonâ-fide holder for a valuable consideration he can only defend by showing that the paper was void.' And in State Bank *v.* McCoy (69 Pennsyl. St., 204) reference is made to Lord Tenterden's ruling in Sentance *v.* Poole (3 Car. & P. 1) that the note of an insane person, or of one perfectly imbecile, which he has been induced to sign by fraud and imposition, is void in the hands of an innocent indorsee, but that it does not follow that a note given by an intoxicated person is void in the hands of a holder for value without notice of the maker's condition when it was given. In that case accordingly the defence was not allowed, as to hold otherwise when nothing showing fraud appeared on the face of the note would retard the usefulness and negotiability of such documents. (*Cp.* Pollock *v.* Burns, 2 Rettie (Sco) 497, and see especially the Bills of Exchange Act, 1882, § 22.) The case of *necessaries* may also under certain circumstances be an exception to the general rules of law. Thus Pollock, C.B., in Gore *v.* Gibson (13 M. & W. 625), says: ' A tradesman supplying a drunken man with necessaries may recover the price if the party keeps them when he becomes sober, although a count for goods bargained and sold would fail.' To the same effect are the words of Alderson, B., in the same case (626), who, however, seems to think it is necessary that he acquiesce when sober, for he says, ' I doubt whether if he repudiated the contract when sober any action would lie upon it.'

I. How far a Drunkard's Contracts may be ratified.

The last point which need be noticed is that the contract of a drunken man has been held to be not void *ab initio*, but only voidable. (*Cp.* Pollock, C.B., in Matthews *v.* Baxter, L. R. 8, Exch. 132.) A drunkard's contract can therefore be ratified by him when he is sober, and that notwithstanding that his intoxication was complete at the time of contracting. (*Cp.* Alderson, B., in Gore *v.* Gibson, 13 M. & W. 626.) The principle prevailing in such cases is that by the ratification, express, or by conduct, there arises an implied contract to pay for the goods (Alderson, B., id. ib.). On this point we may quote the words of Kelly, C.B., in Matthews *v.* Baxter (L. R. 8, Exch. 133). 'It has been argued that a contract made by a person in the position of the defendant is absolutely void. But it is difficult to understand this contention. For surely the defendant on coming to his senses might have said to the plaintiff, " True, I was drunk when I made this contract, but still I mean now that I am sober to hold you to it;" and if the defendant could say this, surely there is a reciprocal right in the other party. The contract can't be voidable only as to one party, but void as to the other, and if the drunken man comes to his senses and then ratifies it, I think he is bound by it.' In the same case Martin, B., spoke to the same effect: 'I am of the same opinion: though the judges in Gore *v.* Gibson used the word " void," I can't think they mean absolutely void. They simply mean a drunken man's contract can't be enforced against his will. But it does not follow that it is incapable of ratification.'

2.—ENGLISH LAW IN CRIMINAL CASES.

However considerate English law is in protecting persons from the effects of injudicious contracts into which they may have entered while in a state of intoxication, it certainly does not afford the same relief to those who happen while intoxicated to commit acts which are considered to be torts or crimes. As Alderson, B., says in Gore *v.* Gibson (13 M. & W. 624): 'There is a material distinction between what a drunkard does against another *in invitum* and what a party does with respect to him by way of contract, knowing him to be drunk.' So in Prentice *v.* Achorn (2 Paige 30, New York R.) the Chancellor said: 'Voluntary drunkenness will not protect a person from liability for torts or from punishment for crimes committed while in that situation,' and in Barrett *v.* Buxton (2 Aikens 167, Vermont R.) it was said: 'As it respects crimes or torts, sound policy forbids that intoxication should be an excuse; for if it were, under actual or feigned intoxication, the most atrocious crimes and injuries might be committed with impunity.' The law in its full strictness is laid down by Hawkins ('Pleas of the Crown,' ch. i., § 6) thus: 'He who is guilty of any crime whatever through his voluntary drunkenness shall be punished for it as much as if he had been sober.' So Hale, P. C. 1, 15, § 32, says: 'This vice (drunkenness) doth deprive men of the use of reason, and puts many men into a perfect but temporary frenzy; and therefore, according to some civilians, such a person committing homicide shall not be punished simply for the crime of homicide, but shall suffer for his drunkenness answerable to the nature of the crime occasioned thereby, so that yet the formal cause of his punishment is rather the drunkenness than the crime committed in it; but by the law of England such a person shall have no privilege by this voluntary contracted madness, but shall have the same judgment as if he were in his right senses.' (*Cp.* Plowd, 19 a, Crompt. Just., 29 a.) And Coke upon Littleton, 547 a, speaking of persons *non compos mentis*, says: 'As for a drunkard who is *voluntarius dæmon*, he hath (as hath been said) no privilege thereby, but what hurt or ill soever he doth, his drunkenness doth aggravate it; *omne crimen ebrietas et incendit et detegit.*' So, too, in the fourth book of 'Blackstone's Commentaries,' p. 25, it is laid down that our law looks upon intoxication as an aggravation of any crime committed whilst under its influence rather than as an excuse for any criminal misbehaviour; and Lord Bacon says: 'If a madman commit a felony he shall not be excused because his imperfection came by his own default' (Bacon's Works, vol. iv., p. 36). In one case it is even said to have been held that 'if the insanity were the offspring of intemperance and the person *knew* that intoxication would produce it, he could not plead it as an apology' (Balfour Browne's 'Medical Jurisprudence of Insanity,' p. 251). In fact, the law of England in respect to the criminal responsibility of drunkards was not dissimilar to that of ancient Greece, where, according to Puffendorf (B. viii., c. 3), 'the law of Pittacus enacted that he who committed a crime when drunk should receive a double punishment, one for the crime itself and the other for the inebriety which prompted him to commit it.' But Roman law was on the other hand far more lenient, and admitted drunkenness as an excuse for crime; at all events, in the Digest (49, 16, 6, 7) it is said, treating of punishments on soldiers for breaches of military discipline, *per vinum aut lasciviam lapsis capitalis pœna remittenda est.* The reason as given in

Stephen's 'Commentaries,' vol. iv., p. 30, for the stringency of the English law, is that the latter, 'considering how easy it is to counterfeit this excuse, and how weak an excuse it is (though real), will not suffer any man thus to privilege one crime by another, and it is an offence of itself to be found drunk and disorderly in any public place.' On the last point we may refer to the two statutes, 4 Jac. I. c. 5 and 21 Jac. I. c. 7, by which a person convicted of drunkenness could be made to pay a fine to the churchwardens of the parish, and in default thereof be put in the stocks; to 13 Car. II. c. 9, by which seamen are made punishable for drunkenness by fine, etc., as the court-martial shall think fit; and lastly to the statute which now regulates such offences, the Licensing Act of 1872 (35 and 36 Vic., c. 94), by § 12 of which every person found drunk in any highway or other public place, whether a building or not, or on any licensed premises, shall be liable to a penalty not exceeding ten shillings, and on second conviction within a year to one of twenty shillings, and a third or subsequent conviction to one of forty shillings, while riotous conduct of drunken persons in public places or when in charge of carriages, horses, etc., is punishable by a penalty not exceeding forty shillings, or imprisonment with or without hard labour for a term not exceeding one month. (For cases under the Act see Paterson on 'The Licensing Acts,' pp. 20-23.) See also Hawkins, P. C., ch. vi., § 5, where drunkenness is included among offences against religion, and ch. 78, § 20. It is interesting to note also that in France, so far back as 1536, severe edicts against drunkenness were made for Brittany by François I. and his legists, the punishment for a first offence being a term of bread-

and-water diet in prison; for a second, flogging; and in case of incorrigibility, loss of ears and banishment.

A. *Drunkenness not a Criminal Plea.*

For the general rule of English law there is ample case authority. Thus in Rex *v.* Patrick Carroll (1835, 7 C. & P. 145) the prisoner—a royal marine—was charged with murdering a woman who kept a public-house at Woolwich by first knocking her senseless and then stabbing her with his bayonet, and though it was proved that he had entered the house in a drunken state, and that the attack was made on his being ordered out, he was found guilty and subsequently executed. Again, in Rex *v.* Meakin (1836, 7 C. & P. 297), the charge was stabbing with intent to murder a constable with a fork, and prisoner said that he was something the worse for liquor, and would not have done it had he been sober, yet he was found guilty of the whole charge. In charging the jury, Alderson, B., said: 'The prisoner's being intoxicated does not alter the nature of the offence. If a man chooses to get drunk, it is his own voluntary act: it is very different from a madness which is not caused by any act of the person.' So in John Burrow's case (York Sum. As., 1823, 1 Lewin's c.c. 75), prisoner, who was indicted for rape, urged that he was in liquor at the time, but Holroyd, J., said: 'It is a maxim of law that if a man gets himself intoxicated he is liable to the consequences, and is not excusable on account of any crime he may commit when infuriated by liquor provided he was previously in a fit state of reason to know right from wrong.'

B. *Unless it amount to Insanity.*

Insanity, however, even when induced by drinking habits, will excuse from criminal responsibility. On this point see especially Mr. Justice Stephen's charge in Reg. *v.* Davis (Newcastle, 27th April, 1881). The prisoner here was charged with feloniously wounding his sister-in-law with murderous intent. It was proved that ordinarily he was well-behaved, and, indeed, was sober at the time of the act, though he had been drinking heavily previously. The medical men who examined him found him suffering from delirium tremens, resulting from over-indulgence in drink, and certified that, though he knew what he was doing, he could not distinguish between right and wrong when he did the act, and that his actions were so little under his control that neither fear of punishment nor legal or moral considerations would have deterred him from it. On these facts Stephen, J., said: 'You will have to consider whether he was in such a state of mind as to be thoroughly responsible for his actions. Nobody must suppose—and I hope no one will be led for one moment to suppose—that drunkenness is any kind of excuse for crime. If this man had been raging drunk and had stabbed his sister-in-law and killed her, he would have stood at the bar guilty of murder beyond all doubt or question. But drunkenness is one thing and the diseases to which drunkenness leads are different things; and if a man by drunkenness brings on a state of disease which causes such a degree of madness, even for a time, which would have relieved him from responsibility if it had been caused in any other way, then he would not be criminally responsible.

In my opinion in such a case the man is a madman, and is to be treated as such, although his madness is only temporary. . . . As I understand the law, any disease which so disturbs the mind that you cannot think calmly and rationally of all the different reasons to which we refer in considering the rightness or wrongness of an action—any disease which so disturbs the mind that you cannot perform that duty with some moderate degree of calmness and reason may be fairly said to prevent a man from knowing that what he did was wrong. Delirium tremens is not the primary, but the secondary, consequence of drinking, and both the doctors agree that the prisoner was unable to control his conduct, and that nothing short of physical restraint would have deterred him from the commission of the act. If you think there was a distinct disease caused by drinking, but differing from drunkenness, and that by reason thereof he did not know that the act was wrong, you will find a verdict of not guilty on the ground of insanity.' In this case, accordingly, the jury brought in a verdict of not guilty. So again, in Reg. v. Baines (1886), Mr. Justice Day ruled 'that, whatever the cause of the unconsciousness, a person not knowing the nature and quality of his acts is not responsible for them,' and in John Burrow's case (*supra*) Holroyd, J., said: 'If, indeed, the infuriated state at which he arrives should continue and become a lasting malady, then he is not amenable.' The American case, U. S. v. Drew (5 Mason, Cir. R. 28) is especially notable. Here a shipmaster was accused of murdering his second mate on the high seas, and the defence of insanity was set up. It appeared that the prisoner had for a considerable time before the act been in the habit of indulging in very gross and continual drunkenness, and about five days before had ordered all the liquor on board to be thrown overboard; he soon afterwards began to display great restlessness and irritability, and could not sleep, and in fact betrayed all the marked symptoms of delirium tremens brought on by drunkenness. Story, J., said under these circumstances the indictment could not be maintained. Even insanity whose remote cause is habitual drunkenness is an excuse for homicide. 'Had the crime been committed while Drew was in a fit of intoxication he would have been liable to be convicted of murder. As he was not then intoxicated, but merely insane from an abstinence from liquor, he cannot be pronounced guilty of the offence. The law looks to the immediate, and not to the remote, cause.' (See also Taylor's 'Medical Jurisprudence,' ii., p. 596, and Archbold's 'Criminal Practice,' p. 19.)

C. But Drunkenness itself is not Insanity.

If the insanity induced be merely momentary, it is very doubtful whether it would be admitted in exoneration. So Earl Ferrers is reported to have said during his trial for murder in 1760: 'If my insanity had been of my own seeking as the *sudden effect of drunkenness*, I should be without excuse.' And in Wm. Rennie's case (Carlisle Spr. As., 1825, 1 Lewin, C.C. 76), where prisoner had urged in mitigation of an offence of burglary that he was drunk, Holroyd, J., said: 'Drunkenness is not insanity, nor does it answer to what is termed an unsound mind, unless the derangement which it causes becomes fixed and continued by the drunkenness being habitual, and thereby rendering the party incapable of distinguishing between right and wrong.' In U. S. *v.* Drew (*ubi supra*) too, Story, J., said the case in which drunkenness does not excuse is when 'the crime takes place, and is the immediate result of the fit of intoxication and while it lasts.' Hallucinations and illusions, also, which are a common effect of drunkenness, do not seem to constitute insanity when so induced. Thus, Marc relates a case where two friends being intoxicated, the one killed the other under an illusion that he was an evil spirit, yet he was condemned to ten years' imprisonment with hard labour, and in Reg. *v.* Patteson (Norfolk Lent As., 1840), where a man while intoxicated had killed a friend under the illusion that he was another person come to attack him, a verdict of guilty was returned on the issue whether, had he been sober, he would have perpetrated the act under a similar illusion !

D. *Drunkenness as an Extenuation of Crime.*

It will be convenient to consider now how far, apart from questions of insanity, drunkenness will be allowed to extenuate criminal acts. On this point we may quote Dr. Paley, who says: 'The only guilt with which he (the drunkard) is chargeable, was incurred at the time when he voluntarily brought himself into this situation; and as every man is responsible for the consequences which he foresaw, or might have foreseen, and for no other, this guilt will be in proportion to the probability of such consequences ensuing' ('Moral Philosophy,' iv., c. 2). If, then, the drunkenness was not voluntarily incurred, no responsibility should attach. So Balfour Browne ('Medical Jurisprudence of Insanity,' p. 312) says: 'If it could be proved that the man had not made himself drunk, if it could be proved that another by force, fear or fraud made him take that which caused his temporary incapacity, then it appears to us to be the best opinion that he would not be held responsible for any criminal act committed by him during the drunkenness, if the intoxication was of such a nature as to preclude the possibility of his knowing what he did.' As tending to show *bonâ fide* apprehension or want of criminal intention, the fact of drunkenness must, too, be very important. Thus Park, J., in Marshall's Case (Lancaster Sum. As., 1830), and in Goodier's Case (York Sum. As., 1831), directed the jury to take into consideration, besides the other circumstances, the fact of the prisoner being drunk at the time, in order to determine whether he acted under a *bonâ fide* apprehension that his person or property was about to be attacked (1 Lewin, C.C. 76). To the like effect are the words of Crowder, J., in Reg. *v.* Gamlen (1 F. and F. 90). So in Reg. *v.* Price (Maidstone Sum. As., 1846) the deceased had in joke sprung upon the prisoner in the dark, and demanded his watch or his life, and the latter, who had been drinking, thinking that his assailant was really a robber, beat him severely, so causing his death. Coltman, J., here said it appeared to be quite clear that the prisoner had acted under the impression that he was protecting his own life from the attack of a robber, and therefore could not be held criminally responsible. The jury accordingly found a verdict of not guilty (Taylor, 'Medical Jurisprudence,' ii. 597). So if the prisoner has through his drinking habits injured his mental capacity, this ought to be taken into account. As Taylor says ('Medical Jurisprudence,' ii. 595): 'When the mind of a man is completely weakened by habitual drunkenness, the law infers irresponsibility unless it plainly appears that the person was at the time of the act, whether of a civil or of a criminal nature, endowed with full consciousness and reason to know its good or evil tendency.' (*Cp.* Humfrey *v.* Maybury, *id. cit.*) So Lord Coke, in Beverley's case (4 Co. R., 123, b), says: '*Non compos* shall not lose his life for felony or murder because *ut pœna ad paucos, metus ad omnes perveniat*, but the punishment of a *non compos* cannot be an example to others; (2) no felony can be committed without a felonious intent and purpose.' And Wightman, J., in the case of Reg. *v.* Doody (Staffordshire Spr. As., 1854), said: 'The question for the jury was whether the prisoner had a mind capable of contemplating the act charged, and whether he did in fact intend to take away his own life. The fact of drunkenness is material in order to arrive at the conclusion whether or no the prisoner really intended to destroy his life. But the mere fact of drunkenness is not in this or other cases of itself an excuse for crime' (6 Cox, C.C. 463). So in the similar case of Reg. *v.* Moore (Sussex Sum. As., 1852), Jervis, C.J., said: 'If the prisoner was so drunk as not to know what she was about, how can you say that she *intended* suicide?' (3 C. & K. 319). *Cp.* Rex *v.* Cruse, per Patteson, J., approved by Coleridge, J., in Reg. *v.* Monkhouse (4 Cox, C.C. 55). We may also here cite a recent Scotch case of Elizabeth Short (Glasgow Circuit Court, 1889). The prisoner was charged with culpable homicide, in that she had neglected to provide necessary food, etc., for her infant son, in consequence of which he died. It appeared, however, that at the time of the neglect she had been almost constantly drunk, and had also had delirium tremens, and Lord Young did not as much as call upon her counsel to plead, saying that no evidence had been brought by the prosecution sufficient to justify a verdict of guilty. He denied that it was murder, culpable homicide, or any crime punishable by law in that court for either a man or a woman to drink too much whisky, or get an attack of delirium tremens, which was insanity. In this case there was no intention to injure, and he must rule that there was no proof of any crime. The jury accordingly found a verdict of not guilty (*Brit. Med. Jour.*, October 19th, 1889).

E. *As showing Want of Premeditation.*

Again, whenever it is material to a charge that *malice* be made out, the jury must take the fact of the prisoner's drunkenness into account. The same consideration, too, will be of weight in cases of assault upon sudden provocation. So in Pearson's Case (Carlisle Spr. As., 1835), Park, J., said: ' Drunkenness may be taken into consideration to explain the probability of a party's intention in the case of violence committed on sudden provocation ' (2 Lewin, C.C. 144); and in Rex *v.* John Thomas (1837, 7. C & P. 817), Parke, B., said: ' Drunkenness may be taken into consideration in cases where what the law deems sufficient provocation has been given, because the question is in such cases whether the fatal act is to be attributed to the passion of anger excited by the previous provocation, and that passion is more easily excitable in a person when in a state of intoxication than when he is sober. So where the question is whether the words have been uttered with a deliberate purpose, or are merely low or idle expressions, the drunkenness of the person uttering them is proper to be considered. But if there really be a previous determination to resent a slight affront in a barbarous manner, the state of drunkenness would not furnish an excuse.' *Cp.* Reg. *v.* Moore (16 Jurist, 750, note) and Rex *v.* Grindley (Worcester Sum. As., 1819). In the second of these cases, where upon a charge of murder the material question was whether the act was premeditated, the fact of the intoxication of the party was holden to be a circumstance proper to be taken into consideration (see ' Russell on Crimes,' 5th edit., i., p. 115). As to this case, however, Park, J., subsequently said : ' Highly as I respect that late excellent judge (Holroyd), I differ from him, and my brother Littledale agrees with me. He once acted upon that case, but afterwards retracted his opinion, and there is no doubt that that case is not law' (Rex *v.* Carroll, 7 C. & P. 145).

Again, where the charge is assault with intent to murder, the jury may find the prisoner guilty of the assault, though not of the intent if he were so drunk as not to have control over his faculties (Reg. *v.* Cruse, 1838, 8 C. & P. 541). But the nature of the weapon used seems to be important here, as Alderson, B., said in Rex *v.* Meakin (1836, 7 C. & P. 297): ' With regard to the intention, drunkenness may, perhaps, be adverted to according to the nature of the instrument used. If a man uses a stick, you would not infer a malicious intent so strongly against him, if drunk, when he made an intemperate use of it, as you would if he had used a different kind of weapon; but where a dangerous instrument is used, which, if used, must produce grievous bodily harm, drunkenness can have no effect on the consideration of the malicious intent of the party.' Again, it would seem that, if a person did a wrongful act, *thinking he had a right to do it*, he would be excused (Reg. *v.* Twose, Exeter, 1879), but whether this lenient view would be adopted when the wrong idea was due to drunkenness is not certain.

F. *Personal Peculiarities.*

In the opinion of some judges, the quantity of liquor consumed is of importance. Thus, Coleridge, J., in Reg. *v.* Monkhouse (1849, 4 Cox, C.C. 55), said: 'Drunkenness is ordinarily neither a defence nor excuse for crime, and when it is available as a partial answer to a charge, it rests on the prisoner to prove it, and it is not enough that he was excited or rendered more irritable unless the intoxication was such as to prevent his restraining himself from committing the act in question, or to take away from him the power of forming any specific intention. Such a state of drunkenness may no doubt exist. To ascertain whether or not it did exist in this instance you must take into consideration the quantity of spirit he had taken, as well as his previous conduct.' So Chief Baron Palles said (Reg. *v.* Mary R., 1887), cited in N. Kerr's 'Inebriety,' p. 395, ' that if anyone from long watching, want of sleep, or depravation of blood, was reduced to such a condition that a smaller quantity of stimulant would make him drunk than would do so if he were in health, then neither law nor common-sense will hold him responsible for his acts.' And Baron Pollock said (Reg. *v.* Mountain, 1888), cited in N. Kerr's 'Inebriety,' 2nd edit., p. 398: 'though at the time an alleged murder was committed (though the prisoner had been a drunkard and had had delirium tremens) he had taken only such a quantity of intoxicating liquor as an ordinary man could take without upsetting his reason, an insane predisposition being the main factor, although the drinking of a small quantity of alcohol was the contributory cause, the plea of irresponsibility was good.'

G. *Some Special Cases.*

It sometimes happens, in the case of crimes against the person and against property, that the prisoner pleads that the person alleged to have been wronged himself consented to the act. The question thus arises, how far the consent of a person in a state of drunkenness excuses a prisoner from an act which, without the other party's consent, would be a crime. This point arose in the case of Reg. *v.* Reeves (Essex Sum. As., 1859). Here prosecutor, being somewhat tipsy, lay on the ground, and while there saw prisoner take his watch, but, thinking that the latter's motives were friendly, he took no steps to prevent the act. Crowder, J., accordingly directed the jury that this was not a case of larceny at common law, but one of bailment; and the jury held the prisoner was not even guilty of conversion as a bailee. But it would seem, although this is a matter of some doubt, that it constitutes no valid excuse in a case of rape for a man to prove that the woman with whom he had intercourse was insensible from drink, and consequently unable to offer effectual resistance (R. v. White, cit., Tidy, ' Leg. Med.,' ii., p. 193). In R. v. Camplin (1 Den., C.C. 89) prisoner gave a girl of thirteen liquor for the purpose of exciting her, and on her becoming quite drunk and insensible he violated her, and it was held that this was rape.

H. Law of Evidence.

If a prisoner has, when drunk, made a statement, the latter is not because of the drunkenness inadmissible as evidence against him (see Coleridge, J., in Rex v. Spilsbury and others, 7 Car. & P. 187). But the jury can in such a case consider his state of mind as an infirmative circumstance (Best on ' Evidence,' p. 669).

So, if a man come forward to give evidence in a drunken state, it will be for the judge to say whether he is competent. In such cases the presumption is in favour of the witness's competency, but if he is undoubtedly drunk he ought to be refused. The real point would be the deficiency of intellect, and that in the case of a drunken person would be inferred from his appearance—*Ebrictas probatur ex aspectu illius qui asseritur ebrius* (Max de Prob. Con. 579). So if one of the jurymen is evidently drunk, the judge ought, in order to prevent the scandal and perversion of justice which would arise from compelling him to act, to order him to step down (Campbell, C.J., in Mansell v. Reg., 1 Dears, and Bell, 405).

I. *How far is Compulsory Control legal ?*

It should be noted that there is nothing in England corresponding to the *curatelle* which is recognised in some countries. So far, however, as Jersey law is concerned, reference may be made to the case *ex parte* Charles Nicolle (P. C. on app. from Royal Ct. of Jersey), L. R., 5 Ap. Ca. 346. But we have a peculiar class of persons created by the Habitual Drunkards Act, 1879 (42 and 43 Vict., c. 19), and a consideration of their criminal responsibility may arise at any time. Prior to this Act the superstitious reverence of English law for the liberty of the subject prevented the exercise of any compulsory control over habitual drunkards. Now, however, it is lawful for one who falls short of lunacy, but is, nevertheless, through the effects of drink, incapable of managing himself and his affairs, to place himself in the custody of one holding a license to keep a retreat under this Act; but only such can apply for admission who are able to understand the full nature of their action, so that the benefits of the Act are refused to those who stand most in need of compulsory control. The law as above stated, then, whether civil or criminal, is not altered so as to give any preference to those who accept the privileges of the Act, and until the restraint of habitual drunkards is made compulsory English law is hardly likely to follow the American in holding that the inquest establishing a case of habitual drunkenness leads to a *primâ facie* presumption of the subject's incapacity to manage his affairs (see Klohs *v.* Klohs, 61 Pennsyl. St., 245).

3.—THE AMERICAN LAW AND ALCOHOLISM.

Great praise and honour is due to the United States for the advanced thought displayed in the world of jurisprudence in relation to the acceptation of alcoholism as a disease and framing legal enactments to meet the necessities of cases arising from causes beyond the control of inebriates. In reality, the English and American statutes are strikingly at variance in understanding and administering the law upon this subject. Perhaps the advantages, from an equitable and humanitarian point of view, attaching to the laws of the United States arise from the fact that until recently the study of diseases due to alcohol was better understood in the Great Republic than in any other country. Clark Bell, Esq., of New York, very ably presents the United States law in an interesting paper as follows :

CIVIL RELATIONS.

Intoxication was regarded by the common law, when complete and characterized by unconsciousness, as a species of insanity. Lord Coke's fourth manner of *non compos mentis* was, '4. By his own act as drunkard.'

Delirium tremens, which results directly from habits of intoxication, is in law considered to be a form of insanity, and this has been repeatedly held by the Courts.

It has always been a well-settled rule of law that no person can make a contract binding upon himself while he is wholly deprived of his reason by intoxication. This would be true as to deeds, wills, all instruments and obligations of every kind.

This rule is not changed, where the intoxication was not procured by the other party to the contract, but is voluntary on the part of the drunkard.

By the common law, as well as by the New York Statute, a testator must, at the time of the execution of a will, be of *sound mind and memory*, and it is as requisite to have the presence of a *disposing memory* as a *sound mind*.

By common law and by statute law, an intoxicated person is thereby rendered incompetent as a witness. The statute law usually classifies such intoxicated persons as lunatics, and the provisions frequently apply similarly to each and to both.

In the marriage contract, which in some respects is treated on different grounds from all other contracts, from the necessity of the case and consequences upon consummation, the sound general rule has been: that if the party was so far intoxicated as not to understand the nature and consequences of the act, this would invalidate the contract.

By English law the Lord Chancellor, as the direct representative of the Crown, has always exercised the right of assuming the custody and control of the persons and estates of all those who, by reasons of imbecility or want of understanding, are incapable of taking care of themselves.

Writs *de lunatico inquirendo* were issued in cases to inquire whether the party was incapable of conducting his affairs on account of habitual drunkenness.

This principle has been exercised and adjudicated

on in Kentucky, in Maryland, Illinois, Indiana, and North Carolina.

The Legislatures of the various States have vested this power by statutory enactments in various tribunals : for example, in New York, by the old law, in the Chancellor; in New Jersey, in the Orphans' Court; in South Carolina, equally in the law and equity side of the Courts; and now in New York, where the distinction between law and equity has been abolished, in the Supreme Court, which exercises it.

In many of the American States the habitual drunkard even is classified and treated under the same provisions, and in the same manner, as the lunatic and the idiot, notably in Pennsylvania, New Jersey, Maryland, Illinois, New York, and many other States.

Taking New York as a fair illustration of the principle, it has been held by the Courts that all contracts made by habitual drunkards, who have been so adjudged in proceedings *de lunatico inquirendo*, are actually void, and that the disability of the habitual drunkard continues after the committee has been appointed, even when he is perfectly sober and fully aware of the nature and consequences of his acts.

It has also been held that *habitual drunkenness*, being established, is *primâ facie* evidence of the subject's incapacity to manage his affairs.

We may then assume, in considering the medical jurisprudence of inebriety, that the law has always regarded and treated intoxication as a species of mental derangement, and has considered and treated the habitual or other drunkard as entitled to the special care and protection of courts of equity, in all matters relating to his civil rights, his domestic concerns, his ability to make contracts, his intermarrying and disposing of his property, by deed, gift, or devise.

The law has gone farther, for it has thrown around him its protecting arm and shield, when it is satisfied that he has become so addicted to drink as to seriously interfere with the care of his estate, and the Courts have then come in and taken absolute control of both the person and the estate of drunkards, in their own interest and for their presumed good.

Medical men should keep in mind the distinction running all through the law between insanity and irresponsibility. The medical view, that irresponsibility should follow where insanity exists, has nowhere been conceded by the law.

CRIMINAL RELATIONS.

(*a*) There are decisions which go to the length of holding that the law will not consider the degree of intoxication, whether partial, excessive, or complete, and even that if the party was unconscious at the time the act is committed, such condition would not excuse his act, and in some cases judges have gone so far as to instruct juries that intoxication is actually an aggravation of the unlawful act rather than an excuse.

But the better rule of law now undoubtedly is that, if the person at the moment of the commission of the act was unconscious and incapable of reflection or memory, from intoxication, he could not be convicted.

There must be motive and intention to constitute crime, and in such a case the accused would be incapable from intoxication of acting from motive.

(*b*) The reasons upon which the rule of law rests may with great propriety be considered, and should be carefully studied before any attempt at criticism is made.

1. The law assumes that he who, while sane, puts himself voluntarily into a condition in which he knows he cannot control his actions, must take the consequences of his acts, and that his intentions may be inferred.

2. That he who thus voluntarily places himself in such a position, and is sufficiently sane to conceive the perpetration of the crime, must be assumed to have contemplated its perpetration.

3. That, as malice in most cases must be shown or established to complete the evidence of crime, it may be inferred, from the nature of the act, how done, the provocation or its absence, and all the circumstances of the case.

In cases where the law recognises different degrees of a given crime, and provides that wilful and deliberate intention, malice, and premeditation must be actually proved to convict in the first degree, it is a proper subject of inquiry whether the accused was in a condition of mind to be capable of premeditation.

Sometimes it becomes necessary to inquire whether the act was done in heat of passion or after mature premeditation and deliberation, in which the actual condition of the accused, and all the circumstances attending his intoxication, would be important as bearing upon the question of previous intent and malice.

(*c*) The New York Penal Code lays down with

precision the provision of law governing the question of responsibility in that State as follows :

Intoxicated Persons.—No act committed by a person while in a state of intoxication shall be deemed less criminal by reason of his having been in such condition. But whenever the actual existence of any particular purpose, motive, or intent is a necessary element to constitute a particular species or degree of crime, the jury may take into consideration the fact that the accused was intoxicated at the time, in determining the purpose, motive, or intent with which he committed the act.

(*d*) Voluntary intoxication, though amounting to a frenzy, has been held not to be a defence when a homicide was committed without provocation.

(*e*) *Delirium tremens*, however, a condition which is the result of drink, and is remotely due to the voluntary act of the drunkard, has been held to be a defence to acts committed while in the frenzy, similar to the defence of insanity.

(*f*) It has been held that, when inebriety develops into a fixed and well-defined mental disease, this relieves from responsibility in criminal cases, and such cases will be regarded and treated as cases of insanity.

(*g*) It may now be regarded as a settled rule that evidence of intoxication is always admissible to explain the conduct and intent of the accused in cases of homicide.

(*h*) In crimes less than homicides, especially where the intent is not a necessary element to constitute a degree or phase of the crime, this rule does not apply.

The practical result, however, in such cases, and in those States where the latter provision of the New

York Penal Code has not been adopted, is to leave this whole subject to the judges who fix the details of punishment. This is a great public wrong, because each judge acts on his own idea, and one is merciful and another harsh. If it is placed by law in the breast of the judges, it should be well defined and regulated by statute. Lord MacKenzie well says: 'The *discretion* of a judge is the law of tyrants.'

4. It will be observed that the law has not yet judicially recognised inebriety as a disease, except in the cases of delirium tremens—above cited—and hardly even in that case.

It is for publicists, judges, and lawmakers to consider the claim now made, that science has demonstrated inebriety to be a disease.

CHAPTER VIII.

TREATMENT OF ALCOHOLISM.

THERE are innumerable obstacles to the successful treatment of any form of alcoholism. Palliation, change of scene, the use of drugs, moral suasion and the deprivation of money, in order to prevent the purchasing of drink, have been tried, and all more or less without benefit. Again, an obstacle is raised to the isolation and independent treatment of most patients from a mistaken sense of kindness and affection. This is fatal to any form of treatment. In some instances, notably where patients can be seen daily by a specialist, and a proper supervision is carried out by an experienced attendant, there can be no hesitation in dealing with such a case at home. As a rule, however, isolation for periods ranging from one to four months in a State or private institution, governed by fixed regulations and properly directed, is desirable for many cases not positioned so as to allow of the treatment being carried out in a well-ordered house.

It must be understood that non-interference by relatives or others is to be a *sine quâ non* in undertaking the cure of a case. Not long ago an American lady determined to place her husband under treatment, but, on finding that the prospective patient must submit to receiving everything at the hands of an attendant, she wavered in her resolution. In my presence the wife admitted that she gave her husband drink if he desired it. In another case the husband idolized his wife, and after agreeing to her detention for three weeks, he broke down in his intention, listened to her entreaties, and took her home. This sort of thing is extremely foolish, and ends in serious mischief. Much care has to be exercised in the selection of nurses and attendants to look after alcoholists. Where this is neglected, the treatment fails in its aim, and discredit may attach to the means employed. In some rare instances it has been discovered that both patients and keepers indulged in orgies that would have disgraced a decent taproom. And it is not an uncommon thing, we are told, for the proprietors of obscure private retreats to lengthen the stay of those under their care by a judicious administration of alcohol betimes, through the medium of subordinates.

In the present state of the law (under the Habitual Drunkards Act, 1879), an inebriate has very little protection unless he is willing to place himself under restraint by his own act. This, it can readily be seen, is a difficult matter to bring about in a majority of cases. What is really wanted is a compulsory clause as a backbone to the present Act. The Act, as it now stands, defines a chronic alcoholist as 'not being amenable to any jurisdiction in lunacy,' and yet he may be beyond all doubt at times dangerous to others, and incapable of directing his or her affairs. The English Government has just appointed a committee of experts and others to investigate the working of the

Act of 1879, and also to determine what punishment or treatment is to be meted out to habitual drunkards.

When we find the Government of the country and influential private organizations pressing for a better understanding of the surroundings and circumstances affecting people subject to chronic alcoholism, or, as it is called, habitual drunkenness, there is evidently a strong feeling permeating all classes to force action of so important a character. The Home Secretary, Mr. Matthews, in speaking of the committee, says: 'Great difference of opinion has arisen as to what kind and degree of punishment for offences committed by habitual drunkards would be the most effectual, both as a deterrent and with a view to the reformation of such offenders. It appears to me that advantage would result from an inquiry being made into the subject.' At last a step is to be taken in the right direction in the important matter of dealing with that irresponsible set of victims, habitual drunkards, who commit offences. The distinction is not a wide one, but it opens up a way through barriers of prejudice and mistaken sentiment which have until the present time been impenetrable.

First of all, let us understand what is meant by an 'habitual drunkard,' and why a man or woman remains so. As we have seen, drunkenness may be a sequence to a bad habit or vicious environment, or it may be transmitted from diseased parents. Do we speak of punishing an insane person? Assuredly not. Then how are we going to draw the line between transmitted insanity and hereditary inebriety? Both come under the denomination of mental disease or change, rendering a man incapable for the time of knowing the possible consequences of his acts. Is the man who enters the world with the nidus of disease latent in his nervous system, either in the shape of a maniacal proclivity to shoot people, commit arson, or to over-indulge in alcohol, to be held accountable for such transmission? There cannot possibly be two opinions as to what the answer would be. Then, why talk of punishment in dealing with these unfortunate people? Are hereditary victims to phthisis, cancer, syphilis, and gout considered fit candidates for drastic measures? And if the law of heredity is accepted as explaining states of disease in one instance, why should others who exhibit a different set of symptoms, yet allowed to be correctly diagnosed forms of disease, the result of heredity, be subjected to different treatment? If anything is to be done, let it be on a fair and settled basis. It is no secret that thousands of families at the present time are kept in a state of terror owing to the conduct of it may be one or more members, victims to the alcoholic habit. As matters stand, redress is difficult. Still, these are the cases that finally contribute to the building up of the criminal calendar. In May of the present year a woman, Jane Cakebread, was charged at the North London Police Court with drunkenness for the two hundred and forty-fifth time!

What a simple story of disease! Yet this woman is treated as a criminal, and her case is repeated daily in the courts of the British Empire. No will-power exists in such people to combat the nervous cry for support and sustenance in the way of alcohol. The expense of keeping 'criminals' of this class under lock and key as a punishment far exceeds in every way the cost necessary to put them through a course of medical treatment with the object of correcting and reforming a depraved system and fitting the patients for some kind of occupation when their state was thought sufficiently improved to allow of their liberty being granted.

As there are two classes of asylums devoted to the treatment and maintenance of insane patients, so should there be asylums or establishments for criminal and non-criminal inebriates. The course of treatment to be undergone, and the period of detention necessary to its being carried out, would be matters for discussion and arrangement on the part of those best qualified to judge of the most efficient means. Habitual drunkards (criminal or otherwise) must be treated as diseased persons. And in helping them, the deprivation of liberty and freedom of action imposed will be found, with properly directed medical treatment, an invaluable aid in building up the physical and mental systems, and in improving the moral tone and, most important of all, strengthening the will-power.

Dr. Pulido, of Madrid, who has just published an essay on alcoholism, does not agree with punishing inebriates in the way of fines and imprisonment, or imposing isolation, whether compulsory or otherwise. He advocates a system of anti-alcoholic education, beginning almost with the child in the nursery. This is well enough as far as it goes! With this he would place the sale of liquor under control, after the Gothenburg plan. Dr. Pulido does not tell us what we are to do with those unfortunates who are now suffering from disease of an alcoholic character. His pretty picture of teaching infants the A B C of temperance principles is all very well; but he appears to overlook the fact that vast numbers of children are being introduced to the world hourly inheriting disease of a kind that no amount of primary instruction, whether beginning with the Alpha of lectures on morals, or ending with the Omega of tuition conveying the strictest of blue-ribbon ethics, can be of the slightest use. Ideals are all very well in their place; but in speaking of conditions of disease and their treatment, an aphorism or a simile would badly replace the assistance of a physician. Dr. Pulido's views regarding the punishment of alcoholists are to be commended, but he is evidently in error in supposing that isolation should never be employed. If by isolation Dr. Pulido means placing a man or woman under lock and key, or submitting the patient to a system of espionage, then I quite agree with him in his objections. In the primary treatment, however, some seclusion is absolutely necessary, and is required by all specialists, but its character need not be of an irritating nature. Tact, discrimination, and trust will do much with such patients. As to the introduction of the Gothenburg system, it is quite easy to understand that its adoption would very materially contribute to the suppression of certain forms of drunkenness.

CHAPTER IX.

TREATMENT OF ALCOHOLISM—*continued.*

THE use of drugs in the treatment of this disease has received a strong impetus within the past two years, more particularly in the United States. The age of healing by faith and suggestion appears to have been resuscitated with all the vigour which characterized similar attempts at influencing the body through the mind which were the basis of the alchemists' power of the Middle Ages. About five centuries ago a noted adept in alchemy, Roger Bacon, gave out to a credulous and not over-intelligent world that at last the philosopher's magic stone had been found, and that through its aid he had been enabled to discover and lay before mankind his celebrated *aurum potabile*, or essence of gold. It was described as the true elixir vitæ, possessing powers rendering it capable of making the old and decrepit young and seductive, like Dr. Faustus in the legend. Towards the end of the last century a Dr. Perkins, an American practitioner, made a great sensation by his miraculous cures, effected by means of a pair of steel tractors about four inches long, supposed by the highly imaginative to be endowed with all manner of rare qualities. He did very well indeed, and had he been content to remain in America, where he made an enormous fortune, posterity might have canonized or lauded him in some fantastic style. He chose to come to England, where his success was almost equal to his Transatlantic fame. Unfortunately for him, a Manchester physician invited a few medical friends to witness some remarkable cures he was obtaining by the use of a pair of pliers fashioned on the plan of those used by Dr. Perkins. Great surprise was expressed at what was seen, and when it got abroad the English physician was delighted to reveal the secret of the miracle. He procured two pieces of wood, passed a rivet through them, and painted them over to appear as much as possible like the genuine article used by the Cagliostro Perkins, and in this way was the collapse of the 'boom' brought about. The original pliers I inspected when in Boston in February last. They are in the possession of Dr. Albert Day. There is a fascination about the word 'gold' which appeals not alone to the imagination, but also to the 'common sense' of the most practical of mankind.

This, perhaps, was not unknown to the latest modern convert to alchemy. I would speak of Dr. Keeley, of bichloride of gold notoriety, resident at Dwight, Illinois, United States of America. For many years he sold his remedies through the medium of the Far West press, and very likely with a commensurate amount of luck in making money. Anyhow, he has run an institute with great success. Later on the star of Fortune attended him well and truly, and conducted to his care some erring members of the Fourth Estate who evidently had not taken to heart Shakespeare's advice against putting a thief into their mouths to steal away their brains.

It does not matter very much what induced them to proceed to Dwight; the evidence is satisfactory that they were there. It is certain at least that gold is not the only active principle in the 'cure,' as it was found that symptoms akin to those manifested on the taking of over-doses of atropine and strychnine were observable. This was a small matter, and at the end of a few weeks the literary men returned to the world without desire of any kind for drink, or apparently so.

One case treated was that of Colonel M., a veteran soldier and an old journalist, who made a sojourn in the Dwight institution. Before going to Dwight Colonel M. had been for some months under the care of Dr. Blanchard, superintendent of the Home at Fort Hamilton, New York; and it is not known what reason finally determined him to experiment with the Keeley remedy. After remaining in Dwight for some weeks, Colonel M. returned to New York and wrote up in his able journalistic style a description of the treatment. As a result largely of his articles, a number of patients of all classes, but particularly from the professional classes, betook themselves to the village of Dwight.

Many among those who went were not confirmed inebriates; but the fashion had been set to cut down the alcoholic propensity, and inherited and acquired forms of inebriety found themselves side by side applying for cure at Dwight.

Numbers of these men were already cured by the mere fact of making a journey of perhaps a thousand miles and then voluntarily remaining from three to six weeks. It must be admitted that the scene presented to my view during a visit to the place in January was most weird and remarkable. Several men were being injected with some fluid, and were given a mixture to take every two hours. Many of them wore glasses, this may have been due to atropine. Several journals in America have, at times, condemned the treatment from different standpoints. If Keeley used water only as an injection, with the rare combination of no drink being allowed to be sold in Dwight and a three weeks' sojourn, would his success be greater? As it is, he has followed lines indicating that where disease did not exist success may have been obtained through an appeal to mental suggestion, and changing the environs. He may claim commercial credit for the systematic and tactful way in which he has worked up his business, which is now in the hands of a trading company. His methods are very irregular and do not invite sympathy; but his knowledge of human nature has taught him to appeal to the psychic or imaginative side of man—that which creates doubt and involves mystery. In doing this, he has suggested hope and opened the door for faith to enter. And what is popular medicine without faith? Had a regular physician made a discovery based upon incontestable scientific data and research, his efforts would have outlasted criticism, and he would have doubled his chances of successfully introducing it to the world. Here we have a man, who is without the pale of the Æsculapian principles, owing to his method of treatment (which is past the experimental stage), and cannot therefore be recognised. He imperils no professional status, and, like a clever man of trade, offers a commodity of some kind that is being looked for by crowds of enthusiastic customers, who in the first burst of gratitude extol—as did the gentlemen of the press—his remedies as a perfect cure. It is regrettable to know that Colonel Mines, who contributed to create the Keeley 'boom' more than any combination of newspapers in America, did not live long to enjoy his supposed immunity from alcoholic attraction.

In September, 1891, certain articles were published in the *North American Review* under the title of 'Is Drunkenness Curable?' written by Drs. Hammond, Crothers, Carpenter, and Cyrus Edson. In the following month Colonel M. printed in reply an article headed 'Drunkenness *is* Curable,' and he described in a brilliant and scholarly manner a supposititious cure that had been effected in his own case. *Ægroto dum anima est spes esse dicitur.* Poor M. knew how he had suffered, and with all the force of his splendid intellect he sang his pæan of praise. The article was, unfortunately, the 'swan's song' of its gifted author in a startlingly tragic sense. On November 4th Colonel M. was found lying insensible in the street, the insensibility proving to be due to intoxication. He was taken to one of the city hospitals, where he died on the 5th of November, 1891. In this case it is evident that the Keeley treatment had not brought about a permanent restoration.

In the consideration of any treatment it is, of course, proper to look for a certain proportion of deaths. One of the Keeley patients, Mr. F., a man not over thirty, never recovered health or spirits after the treatment and died suddenly on Febuary 13th. Mr. E. died in the same autumn, violently insane, after returning home from one of the Keeley institutes. The foregoing represent but a few from a number of prominent men whose deaths followed the treatment. The history of less well-known patients rarely comes before the public. There appears, however, to be sufficient evidence for the conclusion that the use of the so-called Bichloride of Gold Cure is not devoid of danger and risk.

CHAPTER X.

TREATMENT OF ALCOHOLISM—*continued.*

A MATTER of importance in undertaking the cure of any of the varieties of alcoholism is a consideration of the temperamental peculiarities of the patients. It would hardly be intelligent treatment to put a man or woman of, say, a sanguine temperament upon the same footing as patients possessing a phlegmatic or nervous form of constitution. And in dealing with these cases generally, there would be little use in applying treatment to the cure of a drink-crave or disease without first of all dealing with any local or constitutional trouble that might coexist. The latter is a factor likely to be overlooked, occasioning disappointment to the physician and friends by its interference with the success of whatever treatment may be instituted for the alcoholic disease. As for instance, if a man is suffering from an exhausting discharge, is consumptive, is of a gouty diathesis, has suffered from ague, is poorly fed and clad, and perhaps anæmic, has a cancer, is recovering from a prolonged illness, has smoked heavily, been affected with syphilis, or in any way is exposed to a strain upon his natural resources, then it would be futile to attempt to relieve one condition without treating the other. Women are prone to suffer from uterine and ovarian diseases, want of better air, keeping children too long a period at the breast, debility from excessive child-bearing, and unsuitable clothing apart from organic troubles. Children who have been accustomed to take liquor of any description should, without any hesitation, be absolutely forbidden to touch it.

Auxiliaries to the remedies necessary will be found in the employment, according to the requirements of the case, of Turkish baths, hot and cold plunge, and douche baths. The vapour bath is found to be of great service where a tendency to dropsy exists from liver change, and in lithiasis; it also assists in purifying the blood by its action on the skin. Massage, where carefully applied and carried out, proves valuable; and there are very few cases in which it cannot be applied. It tends to improve the tone of the system generally, is advantageous in increasing nutrition, and helps to relieve local congestions. Electricity may be looked upon as a very helpful agent, but its use must be attended by great caution and it should only be applied under skilled direction. Hypnotism has been successfully used, and where hypnosis is attainable through the medium of a competent and responsible operator, very good results can be looked for. Dr. Howard, of Baltimore, relates the cure of two cases amongst others by this method, as follows:

Case II.—Young married lady, aged twenty-nine years; when first seen at Southampton, Eng., was taking morphine hypodermically, gm. 2.5 daily; also alcoholic stimulants, on the advice of her physician in Paris, who had been trying to cure her of morphinomania, as had also several London physicians. She was normally a highly neurotic person, and exhibited mono-symptomatic hysteria, with at times some of its general symptoms, as insomnia, anorexia, dyspepsia, and neuralgic affections, since twelve years of age. She had tried reducing the doses daily, and before she had become such a slave to the drug, had of her own will left it off suddenly. But the horrible torture she underwent in both cases was more than she could bear, and she returned to her nepenthe. She was willing to give up the habit if it could be done without repeating those old tortures, otherwise she would prefer to remain and die a morphinomaniac. The question now arose, "Is she a good subject?" for, remember, subjects are difficult to find at random. The second time I saw her I produced a slight hypnosis, and upon informing the family that I thought I could cure her, they readily consented to place her in my charge. It was a hard fight at first, the hypnosis not lasting over an hour at a time, and would have to be produced again, or the pitiful cries for morphine or brandy would come, and the foundations of the cure would have been pulled down. Gradually she became a good subject, until I could produce a hypnosis lasting seven or eight hours. All this time I was giving small doses of the bromides. By suggestions, after I had gotten her into a "mere state of passivity," she would eat heartily; and after two months of eating and sleeping well without any stimulants, with the promise to see her at any time should her "state of passivity" not last, I returned her to her friends a different woman.

Case IV.—Young married woman, taking two quarts of brandy a day, and any other stimulant she could obtain. Had been a subject for some months. Had kept her from her old habits fairly well, but was unable to see her as often as was necessary. Not having seen her for some weeks, she surreptitiously obtained a quantity of brandy and returned to her old habits. Delirium tremens came on suddenly, and several local physicians were called in. I was telegraphed for, and when I arrived found her in a raving delirium. As I opened the door to her room, where she was smashing things generally, she gave one look at me, stopped her ravings, and at my suggestion lay down upon the bed and slept calmly for eight hours. I was able for the first time in this case to give her post-hypnotic suggestions, and from the time of awakening up to the time of writing castor-oil is more agreeable to her than brandy.'

Every conceivable sort of combination has been suggested for the eradication and cure of alcoholic disease, ranging from croton-oil to morphia in the way of drugs on one side, to extract of frogs and a vegetarian diet on the other. So far, the results are not reported to be strikingly favourable. Prayer and a desire for religion are claimed by the New York Christian Home as the first essential to a cure; and their statistics most certainly point to the success of the lines adopted in that very ably-conducted institution, of which the superintendent, Mr. Chas. A. Bunting, is the energetic head.

The place on my visit had a peaceful charm about it, so monastic in its character that it produced a pleasing sensation of tranquillity and rest.

A primary element to be desired in the treatment of a case is to encourage and support any wish on the part of a patient to be relieved and cured. The enlightenment and fortification of the little will-power left to a sense of the importance to be attached to its strengthening carries the alcoholist a long way on the road to recovery. Moral tone must be given to a patient by every kind of suggestion and impression. Faith clinging to a rock is not more anxious than the unhappy victim of any form of intemperance. At times he fully realizes his condition, and would gladly shake off the frightful octopus that is slowly carrying him beneath the waters of death. But the will is sapped or so weakened that its power for resolve is gone. Hold out every possible hope to a person so circumstanced, and, with care and well-ordered treatment, the alcoholic wreck may be redeemed from its abyss of degradation and disease. Physical force, isolation (excepting at first), threats, and abstraction of sympathy are all out of place in dealing with this form of affliction.

I will now proceed to detail the line of treatment I adopt, together with the remedies in vogue in other countries.

The preliminary step is to ensure that a patient is not in a position to obtain alcohol. Following this, for two or three days the patient should remain indoors (in the case of ladies I prefer that they should stay in bed), and medicines directed to the free purgation of the bowels without exhaustion are indicated, such as saline laxatives combined with a compound cathartic pill. At the same time poultry, broths, or oyster soup, with weak tea, and, if absolutely necessary, one ounce of whisky or brandy daily (but not for a longer period than seven days), may be allowed;

smoking need not be prohibited. Having cleared the stomach and bowels, the patient may be given the following prescription:

    ℞. Tinct. nucis vomicæ - - ʒj.
         Tinct. lavandulæ co. - ʒij.
         Infus. chiratæ -   ℥ij.
         Aq. dest. -   - ad fl. ℥v—℥vj.
    S. One-sixth part thrice daily.

Continue this for four or five days. Should there be restlessness at night, bromide of potassium, or that salt in combination with chloralamide, will be found efficacious. Exercise in the daytime should be permitted, and if the man is being treated in his own home there are many ways in which he can occupy himself. During the whole course of treatment, however—and this applies to both sexes—abstention from intercourse is desirable. If the sleeplessness should continue, the following prescription will be found very useful:

    ℞. Paraldehyde   ʒj—ʒij.
         Syrup. aurantii   - ℥ij.
         Aq. dest. -   ad ℥vj.
    S. A fourth part to be taken every two hours; but on no occasion must more than three doses be taken the same night.

Half a drachm of deodorized tincture of opium may be added to the above with benefit. On the termination of the fifth day the patient should be put on the following prescription, and kept to the same for two or three weeks:

℞. Manganesii sulph.   - ʒj.
    Acid. hydrochloric. pur   ʒij.
    Acid. nitric. pur   - m. xv.
    Auri et sodii chlorid.   - grs. xij.
    Liq. ferri perchlorid.   ʒij.
    Glycerini   ʒj.
    Aq. dest.   ad ℥vj.
S. Half a drachm to be taken every three hours when awake, in a wineglassful of water.

Strychnine is sometimes added to this formula, according to the nervous symptoms that may be present.

The gold frequently causes an irritating red rash to break out all over the body after a week or two. This is not important, and soon subsides. It is, however, an indication of aurism, and suggests the reduction of the quantity of the drug still to be administered.

A combination that may be given in cases where the manganese and gold do not agree, and which has been productive of success, is the following:

℞. Liq. ferri chloroxidi   m. xx.
    Liq. bismuthi et ammon. citratis - m. xx.
    Liq. strychninæ hydrochloratis   m. iij.
    Aq. dest.   ad ℥j.
S. Take three times daily.

This prescription can usually be given for several weeks.

Here is another which I have found a very useful remedy, particularly where liver involvement was prominent:

R. Liq. euonymin. c̄ pepsinâ ʒss.
Tinct. hydrast. - m. x.
Acid. nit. hydrochl. dil. m. vij.
Infus. chiratæ ʒj.
Aq. dest. - ad ʒj.
S. Take three or four times daily for one week, to be followed by an iron tonic.

A good form in which to give manganese iron, and nux vomica is represented by:

R. Manganesii phosphatis gr. xvj.
Acid. phos. dil. ʒj.
Syrup. ferri phosph. ʒiv.
Tinct. nucis vom. - ʒij.
Aq. dest. ad ʒvj.
S. Two drachms four times daily in a little water.

There is little risk in giving manganese in the doses indicated. At the same time it must not be lost sight of that some constitutions do not appear to tolerate the drug in a satisfactory manner. Any of the extreme symptoms, such as adipose changes, loss of nervous power, wasting, etc., never appear except where large doses have been kept up for a long period.

Speaking of hypnotics, I must confess that I now prefer to use hyoscine (not hyoscyamine) in most cases, in hypodermic doses ranging from $\frac{1}{150}$th to $\frac{1}{100}$th of a grain. It is better to repeat the injection than to start with a large dose.

There are some patients who do very well on injections of strychnine. Professor Portougaloff, of Samara, Russia, who has had much success with it, having treated over 500 cases, uses the nitrate of strychnia in chronic alcoholism, delirium tremens, and ebrietas. In his letters to me he says: 'In cases of confirmed habit of taking one, two, or three wineglasses of spirits before meals, up to several bottles during the day, and also in cases of alcoholic poisoning, I always turn to strychnine. I prepare the solution by taking 1 grain of strychnine and dissolving it in 300 drops of aqua destillata, and commence by injecting hypodermically 10 drops of this solution morning and evening in the vicinity of the stomach or liver. I do not order at once to discontinue drinking.' He makes from one to five injections daily. The total number of injections usually made is from twelve to twenty, and they increase in strength from 5 to 10 drops. This represents his treatment.

It must be admitted that strychnine, when carefully used—as it would be in the hands of the eminent Russian specialist—has produced very striking results; and I must say that it is one of the drugs I resort to where I find the iron manganese or gold does not suit. In Germany, at Leipsic especially, much success has attended the use of strychnine. In Berlin also it is now being used with marked success.

The Parisian physicians favour nitrate of strychnine, which was first used in France by Dujardin-Beaumetz and Luton.

To Italy is due the honour of bringing the drug into notice, Dr. Giacomini being the first physician to administer nitrate of strychnia.

Strychnine may be given for three or four weeks,

diminishing the dose gradually, whilst keeping an eye on symptoms of nerve excitation.

Portougaloff makes the following interesting statement: 'I have cases of relapse—patients who once a year return to their old bad habits, but who on such occasions always come to me for a repetition of the treatment, which invariably sets them right for another year.'

As an injection (hypodermic) this may be tried:

 ℞. Strych. nitrat. -   gr. ij.
   Glycerini - - ʒij.
   Aq. dest. - - ʒvj.
 S. Inject 5 drops at 8, 12, 4 and 8 o'clock daily.

The effect of strychnia at all times requires watching, more especially so in cases of heart debility.

Dr. Hammond, Surgeon-General, United States of America (retired), treats the general state, adopting sedatives or tonics where demanded. He also favours the use of baths, electricity, and massage. His sanatorium at Washington is one of the finest in the United States.

Dr. Denison, of Denver, Colorado, has used soda and gold for some years, with satisfactory results. He favours the hypodermic method. He injects the drug twice daily in $\frac{1}{15}$th of a grain doses.

In Philadelphia, Dr. Weir-Mitchell, the noted specialist in nervous diseases, informed me that he considers it highly necessary to prepare his patients for treatment by first attending to the stomach, and imposing rest (more particularly in the case of ladies) in bed for a few days. He considers strychnine useful in alcoholism. In nervous diseases he has used gold for years. Where insomnia is present, he prescribes doses of hyoscine equal to $\frac{1}{100}$th of a grain. Occasionally he uses sulfonal.

Dr. J. C. DaCosta is an advocate of the use of strychnine. He insists on the will-power being cultivated by patients, and gives tonic medicines freely.

He has had fair success with cocaine, giving doses of $\frac{1}{12}$th to $\frac{1}{16}$th of a grain by the mouth. In cases of delirium tremens, 10-grain doses of sulfonal proved of great service. He looks upon cocaine as a powerful diuretic, stimulant, and anæsthetic. After all, however, he relies upon strychnine as the sheet-anchor.

Dr. Walsh, Washington, found that soda and gold did not stop the drink appetite, although it was noticed that the tone of the body was improved.

Dr. Bovee, Washington, visiting physician to the alms and workhouses, gives:

℞. Strych. nitrat. - gr. j.
Ext. erythrox. co. fl. ʒss.
Ext. cinchonæ fl. - - ʒi.ss.
Glycerini - ʒj.
Aq. ad. ʒij.

Sig. Take one teaspoonful every two hours for three weeks.

Also—

℞. Auri et sodii chloridi gr. $\frac{1}{15}$.
S. Inject hypodermically four times daily.

In Canada tincture of hydrastis is considered almost a specific. The dose is 15 minims taken five times daily in half a wineglass of water.

Dr. J. G. Jewell, San Francisco, who has had an extensive experience as a specialist, having treated nearly 18,000 cases, believes in the fluid extract of cinchona (red), and gives one drachm night and morning. This is continued for two or three weeks. Compound cathartic pills are sometimes given. As a hypnotic, bromide and chloral (30 grains of each) are ordered, to be reduced the second night to half that quantity. Electricity is employed in cases of prostration, and the patient is put on a generous diet and acid phosphate. Dr. Jewell is now very partial to the strychnine injections, and considers that the best form of treatment. Some of his cases (not from strychnine) have exhibited very bad symptoms, the pulse not infrequently running down to 42 and the temperature registering below 97° F. He requires patients to remain at least thirty days under treatment. A pill of quinine and strychnine makes a good tonic, and is in much favour with him.

Dr. McNutt, professor in the medical department of the University of California, prescribes tincture of hyoscyamus and tincture of cinchona in treating alcoholic cases.

Dr. Edmund Andrews, the leading surgeon in Chicago, uses prescriptions similar to those employed by Dr. J. L. Gray, of La Porte, Indiana, as follows:

℞. Auri et sodii chlorid.   grs. xij.
    Ammon. muriat. - - - grs. vj.
    Strychniæ nitrat.   gr. j.
    Atropiæ   -   gr. ¼.
    Co. fl. ext. cinchonæ   ʒiv.
    Fl. ext. coca   ʒi.
    Glycerini   -   -   ʒi.
S. Take one teaspoonful every two hours.

Also—

℞. Auri et sodii chloridi - gr. x.
　Strych. nitrat. - - - gr. ij.
　Glycerini - - - ℨij.
　Aq. dest. - ℨvj.
S. Inject hypodermically five drops every four hours, or four times daily.

(This is a singular combination of drugs, and presents features of incompatibility and antagonism. However this may be, the physicians prescribing it claim striking success from its use. The rationale of using remedies of so pronounced an order as atropine, etc., is to affect profoundly the entire nervous system.)

The patients are seen four times daily, and the gold and strychnine are rapidly increased until the symptoms show that the patients are getting all they can well stand. Whisky is given to them. This treatment is carried on from three to six weeks. Dr. Gray has treated over 200 cases. His impression is that about 70 per cent. are cured.

If we are to accept the statements made almost daily in the American and other newspapers as to the vast number of relapses that follow the numerous secret 'gold' cures at work there, and this altogether outside of the list of cases of insanity that are spoken of, is it not a strange thing that systems to whose agency deaths are attributed should be allowed so much freedom from all control on the part of the constituted authorities?

In Great Britain it has recently been settled that all patent or secret remedies are to be labelled 'poison,' if drugs of a character entitling them to be brought under the provisions of the Poisons enactment are present.

England now has a quintette of 'gold' cure establishments, introduced during the last few months by enterprising Americans, with perhaps a sprinkling of Britishers. There is little doubt about one thing, and that is the people will, if they suspect they are neglected, take any remedy, whether advertised or not. The supineness exhibited in dealing with alcoholism as a disease on the part of the profession, and in its legal phases by the Government of the country, has left a loophole for the introduction of remedies that cannot for a moment receive the imprimatur of the profession.

The treatment of alcoholists demands more than a passing attention, and the time appears to have arrived when the claims of that unfortunate class should receive it. The increase in the consumption of stimulants and the appearance of larger crops of neurotic ailments appear to go hand in hand. As has been remarked in an earlier passage, this does not reflect upon the healthy adult who consumes daily a fixed allowance of some form of alcohol. It may be suggested to those who are fond of experiments to try cautiously and carefully the effect of atropine in $\frac{1}{150}$th of a grain doses hypodermically once a day in treating chronic alcoholists.

Dr. Lyman, a prominent physician in Chicago, gives narcotics and tonics.

Dr. Pepper, of the University Hospital, Philadelphia, in cases of delirium tremens begins with hydrobromate of hyoscine, grain $\frac{1}{150}$th. This is followed by pepsine preparations. Capsicum is the remedy he uses to replace brandy and other spirits, and the patients are kept in bed for about ten days. In cases of complete intoxication he gives apomorphia, grain $\frac{1}{10}$th. Where collapse occurs in delirium tremens fifteen drops of digitalis are administered every four hours. As a purgative hydrarg. subchloridum is the drug given in most cases. Bromide of potassium and chloral hydrate, 10 grains of each, may be administered to procure sleep. Hot baths and milk diet complete the treatment.

Professor Burggraeve, of Ghent, recommends morphine, curarine, and atropine in conditions resembling those arising from alcohol. Chloral hydrate may be added, if thought desirable.

Dr. Landor Gray, of New York, is against the immediate withdrawal of stimulants under any treatment. He finds quinine useful, with bromide of potassium as a sedative. Rest and good food are indispensable.

In India, at Bombay, strychnine has been in use for some time, and, it is claimed, successfully.

Dr. Albert Day, of Boston, the oldest specialist practising in the United States, and perhaps in the world, insists upon isolation at the outset, and does not agree with purgation to any extent. In delirium tremens he finds morphine quieting and useful, in, say, quarter to half-grain doses. As a tonic in alcoholism, tincture of calumba is efficacious. As he has treated personally nearly 11,000 cases, his experience can hardly be termed a limited one. In delirium tremens the patients are placed in a closed room, and fed with milk, beef-tea, and eggs. During the first or excitement stage, no drugs are given. If a stimulant should be wanted, ammonia or ether is ordered; where hypnosis is necessary, paraldehyde in drachm doses is given every two hours until sleep is induced. As a rule, two doses are enough. He rarely uses hydrate of chloral, believing it to be highly dangerous where the heart is weak. In chronic drinkers vomiting may be looked upon as symptomatic of approaching delirium tremens. Dr. Day relies strongly upon the use of the following prescription in all forms of alcoholism :

 ℞. Manganesii sulph.   ʒj.
   Acid. nitric. - - - ʒj.
   Ferri sulph.   ʒj.
   Pulv. cinnamomi ʒj.
   Sacch. ust.   ʒiij.
   Aq. dest.   ad ℥vi.
 S. One teaspoonful frequently when the crave is on, and in a wineglassful of water.

He is inclined to think that alcoholism is curable if isolation and treatment are maintained sufficiently long. He admits that great difficulty exists in treating the inherited form.

In the territory of Utah, at Salt Lake City, the physicians practising there assured me that it was not at all an uncommon thing for men and women to enter a drug store, purchase strychnine (as they can do), and immediately place some of the crystals in the mouth, as an antidote to a debauch, or to lessen the drink crave. It is also used hypodermically by the profession.

Dr. Blanchard, superintendent of Fort Hamilton Home, treats about 600 cases per annum, and thinks some cases require at least six months' treatment; he believes that if a relapse takes place after a year's medical supervision the future is fatal in such cases. At his home three months' treatment is insisted on. As is well known, a magistrate can commit for six months to this institution, but not for a longer period. If the patient objects, he can claim a trial by jury. Dr. Blanchard has treated thousands of cases. In dealing with recent cases, he gives alcohol every two hours, in quantities varying from one to one and a half ounces. In the whisky he puts ten grains of bromide of potassium with each dose. Digitalis in 10-minim doses is given three times daily; also gentian and strychnine by the mouth. In cases of delirium tremens, doses of whisky, bromide of potassium, and opium (of the latter fifteen minims) are given together and frequently. Cold affusion is never used. Good food, exercise in the grounds (which are very beautiful and extensive), and the ensuring of sleep, sums up the treatment at this well-known establishment.

At the House of Correction, Holmesburg, near Philadelphia, where nearly 3,000 cases of every form of alcoholism have been dealt with during the past seven years, Dr. Geo. S. Robinson, the resident physician, informs me that the prescriptions given below fairly represent the general treatment of the place. For ordinary alcoholism:

℞. Brom. potass. ℨss.—ʒj.
    Tinct. digitalis gtt. v.
    Tinct. capsici gtt. xv.
    Aq. dest. ad ʒj.
S. Take four times daily.

Treatment. 143

Or—

℞.	Brom. potass.	ℨss.
	Tinct. cannabis ind.	gtt. v.—xv.
	Tinct. capsici	gtt. xv.
	Aq. dest.	ℨj.
S.	Take every two hours.	

In cases threatened with delirium tremens, chloral hydrate is added, gr. xv., to either of the above, and is given every three or four hours; or paraldehyde alone, ℨj., every three hours for three doses; or sulfonal gr. v., every hour for four doses. Alcohol and tobacco are prohibited. A generous diet of soups, beef-tea, milk, and toast, with coffee and tea, added to a limited quantity of water, is allowed.

Dr. T. D. Crothers, the well-known authority on alcoholism, superintendent of Walnut Lodge, Hartford, Conn., and one of the ablest alienists in the United States, afforded me every facility for studying the treatment of alcoholism in all its bearings, during my stay at his magnificent retreat for nervous and allied affections. Amongst other points in the treatment he follows, attention is paid to preparing the system by a course of saline cathartics, vapour, hot, and cold baths; this is continued for three weeks. If evidence of ague is shown, quinine is exhibited; if the patient is underfed, cinchona and iron are indicated; where brain-exhaustion appears, arsenic is prescribed; and in cases of specific mischief, bichloride of mercury is employed. Nux vomica is given after a course of the arsenic. Electricity, faradization, and vapour baths two or three times weekly are found useful. Every day hot and cold showers are taken; salt baths are of use in some cases. At times alcohol is given more for the mental effect created. With spirits, opium in 15-drop doses are added. Dr. Crothers believes that cocaine, atropine, morphine, and strychnine may break up the drink impulse, but there is a tendency to cerebral hæmorrhage and heart failure following such a line of treatment. In many cases he has found that the tinctures of iron and cinchona will stop the crave. Sellerina also possesses some merit. Compound tincture of avena sativa is a quieting agent, but its action must be watched. After a thorough and proper course of treatment, the patients regain brain vigour and nerve strength to a surprising degree. Dr. Crothers also uses bromide of potassium, but not extensively, and when he does it is in 100-grain doses, once daily. He considers the action of bromide of potassium cumulative. If the heart is free, chloral is stimulating if given with whisky, but not alone. In all cases of delirium tremens aperients, as calomel, 5 grains, or pil. cathar. co., are given at first. Morphia may be exhibited simultaneously. The first considerations are to get rid of the congestion and acute intoxication. Proceed with Hunyadi Janos, stimulants, and hot beef-tea. Dr. Crothers has had over 3,000 cases through his hands. The percentage of cures in a number of cases after a period elapsing of from ten to fifteen years averaged between 30 and 40 per cent. Large records of such results are known after five to eight years. He is in favour of at least a four months' course of treatment in the majority of cases. Others, however, require a much longer period. He believes that a predisposition to alcohol or other drugs arises from the presence of a mental or neurotic diathesis.

Dr. J. L. Gray, of Indiana, out of a total of nearly

500 cases of delirium tremens treated with whisky, gold, and strychnine, never had a fatality. He prepares the cases by clearing out the stomach with a hypodermic injection of a quarter of a grain of apomorphia. Sleep usually follows this, and then the tonic treatment is proceeded with. He does not use bromide or chloral, but relies upon hydrobromate of hyoscine as a sedative and hypnotic. He looks for permanent recoveries in 70 per cent. of the cases of alcoholism treated.

The Dalrymple Home, near London, has been very successful in treating this disease. Dr. Branthwaite, the resident physician, has been using strychnine in a number of cases with very good results. Of course, this is only one feature of the treatment, which is looked upon as very thorough. The consulting staff includes some of the foremost specialists in this line of practice in England.

In Australia comparatively little has so far been done in the way of specific medication; but there is every reason to hope that this state of things will not long continue. The remedies used have been on the old lines, with, in some places, here and there, the use of the nitrate of strychnia.

Legislation in England has been directed to voluntary admissions only. On the Continent, in America, and in the British Colonies, the enactments contain voluntary and compulsory clauses which apply to all classes. The periods of detention vary from four months to three years. The law requires that the certificates of two medical men, properly attested before a magistrate or judge, must be obtained before an alcoholist is placed compulsorily under restraint.

The right of appeal to a jury or to the Supreme Court is always open, however, where illegality is suspected, or in cases of prolonged detention. Where the patients have means, they are compelled to pay for their maintenance and treatment. As regards the poorer classes, the State discharges their obligations.

N.B.—Though many of the remedies touched upon in this book are not of a character calculated to give rise to untoward symptoms, it cannot be denied that some special drugs are mentioned which can only be prescribed under skilled advice. It must be clearly understood that in all cases a physician should be consulted before proceeding with any of the lines of treatment laid down.

CHAPTER XI.

ADVERTISED NOSTRUMS.

It may be of interest to state that there are four nostrums, or so-called specifics, being advertised extensively, guaranteed to cure alcoholism. The first is the alleged 'bichloride of gold' remedy, sold at Dwight, which, on being analyzed, gives, in the mixture, the following result:

℞. Ammon. muriat.   -   -   gr. j.
    Aloin   -   -   gr. ij.
    Tinct. cinch. co. - -   -   ℨiij.
    Aq.   -   -   -   ℨj.
M. S. Teaspoonful six times daily.

The hypodermic injection used at Dwight shows an analysis of:

℞. Strych. sulph.   -   -   gr. ss.
    Atropia   -   -   gr. ¼.
    Acid. borac.   -   -   -   gr. xv.
    Aq.   -   -   -   ℨiv.

This solution is placed in bottles, coloured yellow, pink, and red, to suit the tastes of the purchasers.

The result of an analysis of the 'Gold Cure' mixture made in July of the present year by an eminent London analyst, disclosed the presence of 27·55% of alcohol. No gold or chlorides were to be found.

No. 2 remedy is called the 'Golden Specific,' and has sold remarkably well. On analysis, antim. pot. tart. (tartar emetic) was found to be the basis of the so-called remedy, with a little colouring matter and a trace of cinchona bark.

The third specific is a recent invention, and has received the appellation of the 'Boston Drug.' This is almost entirely made up of antim. pot. tart. (tartar emetic).

During my recent tour in the United States several experiments were made with antimonial remedies, and some of them were, to say the least, decidedly unpleasant. Not only can the drink crave be thus moderated or stopped, but desire for any kind of food or liquid is interfered with or altered. The solution usually prepared is:

 ℞. Antim. pot. tart. -   - gr. xvj.
  Aq. dest. - -   ad ℥viij.
 S. Of this put two teaspoonfuls into half a pint of the liquor drunk by the patient. This he may take several times daily.

Should stomach irritation arise, opium will allay the symptoms.

The latest idea introduced to the public is called the 'Fisk Gold Cure.' It is on a par with the Keeley nostrum.

INDEX.

A

ACQUIRED form of disease, 17
Advertised nostrums, 146
Alcoholic trance and crime, 41
Alcoholism, 8
American law and alcoholism, 107
Anæmia accompanying alcoholism, 3, 6
Andrews, Dr. Edmund, Chicago, 137
Arabian physicians, 17

B

BACON, Lord, 78, 92
Bacon, Roger, and alchemy, 120
Barr and German statistics, 16
Beard, Dr., on origin of trance, 74
Bell Clarke, New York, 107
Bichloride of gold cure, 121, 146
Binghampton asylum, N.Y., 8
Binz, Professor, Bonn, 3
Bird, Dr. R., East Indian Army, 20, 34
Blackstone's commentaries, 92
Blanchard, Dr., New York, 122, 141
Blood, alterations in, 1
'Boston Drug' specific, 147
Bouzareingue, De, on transmission, 12
Bovee, Dr., Washington, 136
Browne-Balfour on insanity, 92, 99
Burggraeve, Professor, of Ghent, 140

C

CANADA and hydrastis, 136
Carpenter, Dr., on absence of mind, 72, 76
Cerebral automatism or trance, 58
Children's Hospital, Berne, 33
Civil cases, English law in, 78
Coke, Sir Edward, 78, 92, 100
Coleridge, J., on drunkenness as an excuse, 103
Compte, Le, 11
Compulsory control in law, 106
Contracts, drunkenness as absolving from, 79, 87, 89
Coup-de-soleil, 45
Criminal cases, English Law in, 90
Crothers, Dr. T. D., 33, 47, 60, 143

D

DA COSTA, Dr. J. C., Philadelphia, 136
Dalrymple Home, 145
Darwin, Charles, 8
Day, Dr. Albert, Boston, 121, 140
Deeming's case, 46
Déjerine on heredity, 16
Delirium tremens, 95, 107
Demme, Professor, of Berne, 16, 35
Denison, Dr., Colorado, on use of gold, 135

Drunkenness in extenuation of crime, 94
Dujardin-Beaumetz and use of strychnia, 134

E

EDIS, Dr. A. W. on infant mortality, 34
Edson, Dr. Cyrus, on curability of drunkenness, 124
Epilepsy, 45
Esquirol on power of transmission, 13
Evidence of an alcoholist, 105
Exceptional cases in English law, 85, 88, 104

F

FINLAY on blood changes, 7
'Fisk gold cure,' 147
Forgery in trance state, 50
Fort Hamilton Home, N.Y., 9
Franklin Home, Philadelphia, 9
Fraud implied from drunkenness, 80
Friston, Professor, and analysis of 'gold cure,' 138

G

GALL on heredity, 11
Giacomini, Dr., introduced nitrate of strychnia, 134
'Golden Specific' nostrum, 147
Grain, Le, conclusions on heredity, 17
Gray, Dr. J. L., Indiana, 137, 144
Gray, Dr. J. Landor, New York, 11, 140
Grenier on weak intellect, 12
Gull, Sir William, on alcohol, 19
Gyllenskiold on Swedish legislation, 16

H

HABITUAL Drunkards Act, 1879, 106, 115
Habitual drunkard, what is, 116
Hammond, Dr. on heredity, etc., 13, 71, 135

Harley, Dr., F.R.S., 2, 24
Heart, adipose degeneration of, 7
Hitzig on heredity, 33
Home Secretary, The (Mr. Matthews), 116
Horse stealing and trance, 47
House of Correction, Philadelphia, 10
Howard, Dr., Baltimore, on hypnotism, 127
Hughes, Dr. C., St. Louis, on epilepsy, 71
Huss magnus, 3, 10
Hypnotism, 127

I

INCAPACITY inferred from drunkenness, 78
Incapacity, what constitutes in law, 84
India, strychine used in, 140
Infantile form of disease, 32
Inherited form of disease, 10
Insanity and alcoholism, 38

J

JACKSON, Dr. J. Hughlings, on post epileptic disorders, 73
Jewell, Dr. J. Grey, San Francisco, 136

K

KEELEY, Dr., and his alleged 'cure,' 121, 138, 146
Kerr, Dr. Norman, 103, 104

L

LAMARCK on instinct, 11
Lancereaux, on heart changes, 7
Legal relations, 77
Leucocytes and pathological conditions, 5
Licensing Act of 1872, 93
Luton, and the use of strychnine, 134
Lyman, Dr., Chicago, on treatment, 139

Index. 151

M
MANSLAUGHTER in trance state, 52
McIlraith, J. R., and law digests, 77
McNutt, Dr., San Francisco, 137
Medico-Psychological Society of France, on heredity, 16
Mill, John Stuart, and abstraction, 72
Mines, Colonel, LL.D., case of, 122
Mitchell, Dr. Weir, Philadelphia, 135
Morrell, on hereditary taint, 10
Murder, 52

N
NEW YORK Christian Home, 9, 129
New York penal code, 111, 112
North American Review, 124

P
PALEY, Dr., and drunkenness, 98
Pathological changes, 1
Pepper, Prof., Philadelphia, 139
Perkins, Dr., of America, on miraculous cures, 120
Piorry, on transmitted insanity, 12
Portougaloff, Prof., Samara, Russia, 133
Post-mortem examinations, 6
Pulido, Dr., Madrid, 118

R
RAPE and drunkenness, 105
Richardson, Dr. B. W., F.R.S., 2

S
SOLLIER, M. Paul, classification of hereditary form of disease, 17
Somnambulism, 44
Stephen, J., on an alcoholist's responsibility, 95
Suicide, 45
Sweden, effect of enactments, 16

T
TAYLOR'S 'medical jurisprudence,' 97, 99, 100
Testamentary cases and trance, 59
Thompson, Sir H., on alcohol, 23
Thorne, Dr., London, 73
Tidy, Dr. Meymott, 105
Trance case, 58
Trance, phenomena recapitulated, 76
Treatment, 114
Trousseau, 7
Tuke, Dr., on insanity, 12
Tyndal, McIvor, his catalepsy, 43

V
VILLANOVA, Arnold, 18
Virchow, on pathology, 1

W
WASHINGTONIAN HOME, Boston, 9, 10
Wife murder in trance condition, 49

THE END.

Baillière, Tindall & Cox, 20 and 21, King William Street, Strand.

www.ingramcontent.com/pod-product-compliance
Lightning Source LLC
Chambersburg PA
CBHW030254170426
43202CB00009B/744